Praise for

Authenticity Insurance

"Lee Swann is more than a survivor, she's a thriver. In *Authenticity Insurance*, she shares her wisdom earned through the school of hard knocks. For anyone who seeks to overcome great odds and ascend in life, *Authenticity Insurance* offers you the path to achievement."

—Cathy Carroll, author of
Hug of War: How to Lead a Family Business with both Love and Logic

Authenticity Insurance:
Strengthen Your Superpowers and Actualize Your Purpose
by Lee Swann

979-8-88824-760-0

Designed by Suzanne Bradshaw

Published by

◣ köehlerbooks™

3705 Shore Drive
Virginia Beach, VA 23455
800-435-4811
www.koehlerbooks.com

Strengthen Your Superpowers
and Actualize Your Purpose

LEE SWANN

VIRGINIA BEACH
CAPE CHARLES

TABLE OF CONTENTS

PREFACE

Never have I ever met anyone who said they had a childhood dream of working in insurance. If you know someone, I would love to meet them. Listening to stories from trusted mentors, senior leaders, peers, trainees, and direct reports alike, most people I have had the pleasure of sharing an exchange with all say they "ended up" in the industry.

Nevertheless, like many in a conservative workspace, we have witnessed change being a struggle, whether gradual or all at once. We face the lurking generation gap; it is complicated to get those who identify as late millennials, Generation Z, and younger generations to take conservative spaces seriously because of the grave differences in overall life balance and career outlook.

No one wants to work for an employer they do not align with or feel connected to just for a check anymore. We want to work for leaders who genuinely care for employees' personal well-being. We want work we can leave at work to allow us the freedom of quality personal time. And while higher education institutions are not suffering, there is also something to be said about millennials who come with decades of experience but who cannot grow past a certain role because they do not have a fancy degree or an acronym after their name to prove their worth.

So, what do you do when you are stuck? How do you overcome the obstacles of climbing a corporate ladder in a conservative workplace? Who do you turn to when it seems like no one understands your talent and craving for stimulation?

"What do you do when you are stuck?" My way of working through this question is by reflecting and evaluating your needs, wants, skills, and logistics. Rate your happiness based on where you are, and if your score is not where you want it to be, make a change. You never have to be somewhere you do not want to be, and—most importantly—you are in control of you. Write out a legitimate plan to get "unstuck" and execute the plan.

"How do you overcome the obstacles of climbing a corporate ladder in a conservative workplace?" There is no one answer, but my response is to keep pushing no matter what is said or done by anyone else around you. Trust in your potential. Trust in your power. Even in a work environment where employee resource groups and diversity, equity, and inclusion are a primary focus, there is still politics, sadly. Often, it all comes down to who you know. Having a strong network is of the utmost importance—and maintaining those relationships.

"Who do you turn to when it seems like no one understands your talent and craving for stimulation?" You. It has always been and will always be you, and no one else. You are your way out.

If we asked some folks how they thought authenticity fit into a conservative workplace, we would probably get some laughs, scoffs, eye rolls, and other expressions of disbelief. I am here to tell you, though, that trusting your authentic self is how you make it out of being stuck, whether the problem is your mindset or being physically stuck in a position until something better comes along. Not only will you being authentic allow for opportunities and blessings to show themselves to you, but others seeing you thrive in your light will be empowered by your example. Modeling authenticity and believing in your master plan can be far reaching to all levels and transformational for any team.

It does not matter what a person's life plan looks like. It could be to make over six figures, have a spouse and/or kids, live in a nice house, stay debt-free, travel, or just plain old stay out of trouble. Since we are being honest, let's admit that this oversimplified blueprint of a life plan is the bare bones, and there's nothing wrong with that. But a person who knows what they are working toward is more likely to live in their authentic light than someone with no direction at all.

My life plan is not perfect. Part of my plan is to turn my pain into positivity. I want others to learn from my mistakes and believe their authentic self exists. The life you want is out there, whether it's dominating a corporate career or prospering as an entrepreneur. You are in control. It took me a long time to settle with this myself, so do not shame yourself. We all have a story. This is mine.

My background starts as a Jehovah's Witness growing up in a physically, emotionally, and mentally abusive and negligent household. Although I opted out of practicing when I became of age, I do not regret the experience. I was taught how to do research, write scripts, and act out dialogue to articulate my point on any given topic. Because of them, I have over twenty years in writing, public speaking, and stage performance under my belt, with my largest audience being over 4,000 people. Should you happen to meet anyone with a similar background, I suggest you do not sleep on what they can do. Their ministry school and its materials are unmatched. While Witnesses may have mixed reputations, they can be talented people who, in my opinion, just never had anyone tell them there is more to life and it is okay to explore it. Whether the world ends or not, we all have a responsibility to contribute positively while here.

Given the environment I was in, I moved out at eighteen and never looked back. My first job while living on my own was for a 911 center as a call-taker. And while I thank our first responders graciously, I zero out of ten recommend the role if you personally suffer with mental health issues or trauma. The calls you come across are so heavy, they are indescribable. It is one of the most difficult and stressful workplaces.

Tolerance for mistakes was lower than low. You were only allowed three mistakes per year. And the two-year probation period did not help anything. Needless to say, I barely lasted thirteen months. My third mistake was typing an incorrect location at the end of August 2016. I was surprised I made it that long. I accept my wins, and may the universe receive my gratitude for my time there.

Moving to the insurance industry, there were obvious differences. However, the roots were the same. Conservatism and a corporate air ran both environments. Very black and white, minimal gray. The number-one pro was being in a learning environment. Being "allowed" to make mistakes organically nurtured my ability to self-reflect and problem-solve much better than being in an environment where I had to look over my shoulder in fear of termination daily.

Long story short, I have learned so much since the start of my insurance career. With only a finance certification, I was blessed to make a successful vertical climb very quickly, moving seven grade levels in seven years. Along the way, I found a connection to my path and purpose. I believe myself to have many superpowers. Making something from nothing is one. Creating safe spaces is another.

Whenever someone asks why I like being in leadership, my staple response is "for the people." I love creating safe spaces for people. I will never say I "like" working in claims, but I have a special place in my heart for the people because the challenges they face are not easily understood unless you have also worked directly in a claims function. Complaining to partners or friends is not always easy. You need folks who speak the lingo. And unless you have seen the front lines, we might as well be speaking different languages altogether.

On the way to the privilege of holding a manager title, things were not always smooth. From the start of my career, something I always thought was missing in customer service environments was the care for the employee experience. If I ever was given an opportunity to lead, I vowed to ensure no one would share the struggles I had with some of my earlier leaders. If there was a problem within my power to solve, I felt obligated to fix it. It was my job to inspire and empower others around me and thus prove authenticity is acceptable at work.

Based on my experience, when the leader of any team is connected to themselves and presenting authentically, there is only success. Will there be tests along the way? Absolutely. No one ever said success was easy to attain. Whether you are a new leader or well-seasoned with the gray hair or no hair to prove it, if you are looking for a different perspective on how to spark genuine connection within your team or within yourself as an entrepreneur, and you are truly interested in embracing your authentic self for the purpose of developing a transformative leadership style, there is something here in these pages for you.

The mission and voice behind *Authenticity Insurance* will hopefully help you on your personal journey of discovering or rediscovering your natural talents if you have lost your way. As you continue reading, I encourage you to reflect on who you are as it relates to what you do and whether you are aligning with your real purpose. My story will resonate with anyone who navigates leadership (with or without the title) in the jungle we call *corporate* (and real life) as I share views supporting why being authentic at work is possible and why it is a strength you need in your back pocket if "top-tier" talent is how you want to be considered and what you want to attract.

You likely are already harnessing the necessary skills to survive in any environment. Clearly, you have a curious spirit. You are reading something new right now. I am also going to safely assume you understand sacrifice. We all have responsibilities. At one point or another, we have all held a role we did not like just to keep the lights on. We are going to talk about why this route is no longer worth it and why the connection to your authentic self is what will allow your true colors to illuminate your path forward and drive you toward your desired results.

Being authentic is not reckless. It is responsible. Authenticity can be anyone's superpower, and it is possible for it to coexist with professionalism. I'll share some examples of how I worked through undesirable situations and what blessings came forth from embracing who I am to get where I am. I am grateful for every mistake, every win, every failure, every success, every problem, every triumph. I am grateful for everything. And I am grateful for everyone who has been here for the ride.

Realizing authenticity was what was missing from my formula was one of many epiphanies I've had. It is something I wish I honed earlier; however, another belief of mine is that everything happens for a reason. Every lesson you have learned throughout your life was intended for you to learn it in that exact way at that exact time. The results of those learned lessons and the newly developed thick skin is right where your authenticity lives.

Authenticity Insurance is not only about pushing you to be you. It is also about centering around your deep core for a better route in life and leadership, should this be your cross to bear. Authenticity is about bringing out the best in everyone who is exposed to its light. May we all use our authenticity wisely.

You are light. Be light.

Chapter One

Intention

First things first. Ask yourself, "Who am I?"

Why does this matter? Well, if you do not know who you are, how will you articulate yourself to anyone you want to take you seriously? Knowing who you are inside and out is key. It is not only about understanding your personality and what suit or dress looks the best on you; it is also about what you value, what shapes you, what your core looks like to you. When you finally can effectively express the root of who you are as a person, it is easier to identify the kind of business professional and general human being you intend to be in this world.

If you are unsure about how to unpack yourself, this is the perfect time to figure it out. Better to begin than to not begin at all. You owe it to yourself to take time to identify and understand your desires, goals, and master life plan. No one else can do it for you. Plus, when you think about it, no one can take care of you like you. No one can look out for you like you. No one will always have your best interests at heart like you. Self-work is just that. We all need to own our shit.

If you are in a relationship or have a family, before diving deep into yourself, be considerate of where others may be. Everyone will not understand why you want to suddenly do this work, and it may not be accepted at first. Once you are done, though, everyone will be happier and better off. Authenticity is the gateway to inner happiness, peace, and finding your purpose.

There are many questions to ask ourselves as we evaluate how to unlock our authenticity. There is no time to be shy or afraid or beat around the bush. Prepare to be direct, frank, and honest. While change is inevitable and we must evolve to survive, there is always a foundation. We'll lay our foundation by mentioning something adulthood often makes us forget: What brings you joy, and what motivates you?

Once we cross over into adulthood, the moment we all anxiously await as children, thinking we can do whatever we want, we realize reality is a straight shooter. Even if all the adults in the world screamed, "*You will miss being a child!*" to our youths, none of them would believe us. However, now that we are here, we can commiserate. Adulthood is the worst *hood* we have ever lived in, period. It is hard for absolutely no reason at all sometimes. Things happen out of left field, and what do we do? We put on our grown-up pants and return to the battlefield because time waits for no one, and what is staying home, ignoring reality, going to solve?

Even if your adult life has not been so hard (not wishing negatively on anyone), life happens. A close friend moves away. You lose a parent unexpectedly. You're suddenly laid off from your job after years of loyalty and dedication. There is no escaping the things you cannot control, and there will always be things you cannot control.

As children, we do not think about what we can or cannot control. When we talk to our friends now, sometimes we need to be reminded to let go of the things we cannot control—because there is nothing we can do about it. Children only think about having fun and do not have to think about their happiness. Unless you grew up in unhealthy circumstances like me, most children are inherently happy. Childhood happiness could be gained by the simplicity of video games, playing with friends, watching favorite TV shows, literally anything.

When you reflect on your childhood, what were some of the

highlights? Was it the holidays? Maybe your family always splurged on gifts. Did you enjoy your school experiences? Perhaps you were the class valedictorian or the captain of a varsity sports team. Maybe you were considered unpopular and bullied for standing out. What subjects excited you most? Was math a breeze and you had the teacher asking you for help leading the class? Did you enjoy working with classmates, or did you like to work alone?

How about your familial relationships? Did you have close relationships with family (including outside of the immediate family)? What was your friend circle like? Did you have a large group of friends going to the same schools together? Or was your circle more like a small square or even triangle? Hey, no judgment there at all. In high school, I had the same four to five friends the entire four years. To me, it felt safe. You may feel different, and that is okay!

What about role models? Did you look up to anyone or want to be just like someone when you grew up? Were you in any mentoring programs? Or maybe a teacher was that light for you, as they are for many. I have a couple teachers who stand out for me. I would not have made it to graduation day without them. I will never forget my music teacher going to bat for me with my father so I could perform at my graduation. This was a very big deal, someone defending me against my own family. There are no words.

On a funny note, I halfway regret bombing the show after she put forth so much effort on my behalf. For her effort, love, and kindness in what were some of my most difficult years, I am indebted to her forever. She was a strong maternal presence and happened to teach my favorite subject. Her upbringing and background were also very similar to mine, allowing for a natural connection. If you told me I was not a favorite, I would never believe you. My first year in high school was her first year at the school. We grew together, and she watched me grow up and transition to adult life. We never lost touch. No joke, if she asked me to show up and sing with a group somewhere (which she has a few times in recent years), I would do it. *Zero* hesitation.

She helped hone my skills in the thing that brings me joy and motivates me the most out of anything else in life itself. I cannot go one day without music. A lot of people will probably think that's not special. I promise, it is. Real artists understand. When you find something to connect with, there is nothing else. Music is my heartbeat. Everything is off-kilter without it. On the days I do not have my life soundtrack flowing through my headphones, I can feel the internal disconnection. It is for this reason that I can only listen to music with a message. The beat can knock, and the bass can boom all day. If the words do not speak to me in some way, I will not be listening for very long, and I will try everything. I do not discriminate. A hit is a hit no matter the genre or who is on the track, period. I model myself (in thought, not voice) after the late Whitney Houston. If she did not connect with the words written for her, she passed on the track. That is me all the way.

Words hold weight. I believe it is an artist's duty to responsibly influence the masses. Their message should be positive, meaningful, an example for others to follow. We have so much bad in the world already. This is not one of those "too much of a good thing is bad" situations. Quite the opposite. Our world needs more good, now more than ever. Our survival depends on it.

People often forget what brought them joy and what energized them. Again, we did not have to think about it as children. As adults, we have control over our state of happiness. We cannot make everyone happy. And everyone in the whole wide world will never be happy at the same time, not even for five minutes of crossover. The statistics on this do not even exist. I tried to research it and found nothing. Honestly, I am pretty sure we would have already heard about the one day humankind was happy and at peace if it had happened by now. *That* is newsworthy.

Unfortunately, the media does not work this way. You can see the pattern of how news outlets usually look for the worst to create fear and keep control over your thought process, a.k.a. "programming."

TV, internet, music, and books are programming. If you listen, watch, or read, it is programming you. The "news" is designed to show you the most terrible thing happening, and they might occasionally throw in a positive story, such as a Good Samaritan executing a good deed. But it is not the media's fault the world is unhappy. We can control our programming and the direction to take that brings our childhood happiness back.

In tune with this thought, the other half of our question was about motivations. What brings you joy can be what you like to do, such as a hobby, while what motivates you is what gets you out of bed every day. Some folks do not have the luxury of a hobby no matter how hard they fight to make time. Think of motivation as something in front of you daily. Say you have kids. They may be your motivators to keep going to a job you hate.

Is it money? Is one of your motivators to be the cycle breaker in your family? Is being debt-free top of mind? Do you like helping others? Are you looking for recognition or validation? How do you view growth? Do you aim to climb the ladder and break records? Are your children your motivators, ensuring their lives are better than your own? What about being able to take care of your parents when you get older?

Our list of motivations will be different. I say "list" because it is possible to have more than one. However, none of it matters if you do not take the time to write it down. When the plan is in your head, it is still merely an idea. It is not a real plan unless and until it is on paper. This means you are taking the time to program yourself, counteracting what you watch, listen to, read, and scroll through on social media. This is when you think independently and take control of your life. What the news says will not matter. Shoot, your own family's words will not matter. The world could be ending around you, literally little fires everywhere, yet you sticking to your finely documented and designed master plan allows your world to be all gravy or better than most. I highly encourage you to start writing down what is in your brain. Today. Right now. You will not be successful in finding your authentic self without a written plan.

Before you ask, yes, I am a journaling fan. I believe journaling to be *extremely* helpful. My favorite journal so far had 365 daily journal prompts designed to help answer internal questions relating to personal growth and self-love. I loved it because it forced me to reflect and sit with my thoughts. I intentionally forced myself to write in pen so I could not go back and change my answers. I wanted to ensure my programming was balanced and spoke to the authentic person I aspire to be daily.

I haven't finished the journal yet because some questions were hard to answer in the moment. It was also the fact that it had dates, and any time the date on the page did not align with the actual date, I felt behind, like I was failing. I would ruminate for days or even weeks. Sometimes, it took me time to situate my thoughts. I do not shame myself for not finishing it, and it definitely was not a waste of time or energy. If anything, it inspired me to create my own reflection journal specifically aligned to this very book you are reading, titled *The Authentic Leader Journal*. You can get your copy on Amazon to begin your "reprogramming."

If it takes time for you to develop the habit of writing things down, you will get no shame from me. I do not believe in shaming, not to mean I don't still hold people accountable. We all have our struggles, and they are all valid. Writing things down will keep you from forgetting your direction and who you are. Every time you pick up your plan to refresh yourself or add to it, you are just "getting with the program." Do people still say that? If not, I vote we bring it back.

There's another important element to this. While you focus on personal development, ask yourself what you will not tolerate or put up with, your nonnegotiables. We all have them, and these vary. Evaluating this looks like asking questions about core values. Are you family-oriented? Is money the endgame for which you will do anything? Where and what is your line? Can you accept having little work-life balance for a highly demanding role? Will an environment where growth is nearly impossible be satisfactory if you cannot find any other work?

When I asked about your strengths in school, did you discover some of those changing as you aged? What were you bad at then, and have those areas improved? Maybe you have new weaknesses you are working through. Is there anything you just do so naturally, you could do it in your sleep? Does this superpower connect with anything on the job, or is your talent safer and better off in an entrepreneurial space? Are you brave enough to venture out on your own?

Are you capable of communicating with your direct leader about your strengths and weaknesses? Can you identify what type of atmosphere you wish to have and how you will help your team ascertain this environment? Have you thought about how to speak to all the different working styles and personalities coming together, finding each team member's superpower to better optimize productivity? Are the people on your team able to truly be themselves?

What kind of leader do you portray? Are you present? Are you hard and rigid? Are you versatile? Are you flexible? Are you old-fashioned? Are you close-minded? Are you willing to try new things? Do you still have "favorites"? What would your team say about you when you are not in the room? Does your demeanor or disposition bring passion and inspiration? Or do you just want to clock in and clock out, nothing more, nothing less? When your people reach out to you for opportunities, what is your reaction? What are your intentions? Why do you want to be a leader? Why should it be you with power? What do you really bring to the table?

As leaders, it is our responsibility to look at our surroundings much differently than our direct reports. If you are on the front lines, it is of the utmost importance to solve problems and help make your employees' day-to-day life as easy as possible. The idea is to work smarter, not harder. So, if you are not trying to make your people's job easier, you are failing.

To me, this is why we have front-line employees and managers. If one of my employees brings me a problem, it is my job to find a solution, and if I cannot, I speak to peer leaders and higher-ups for assistance. It is my job to think of programs and initiatives to improve the employee experience, to shield them from and extinguish their fires, to utilize my emotional intelligence and discernment while delivering news or information, and to make my team feel supported, valued, engaged, and highly motivated to produce. The old notion of "shut up and do the work" is gone.

If you intend to be a leader, please consider this decision wisely. If you are in leadership just to be paid, I judge you. Does this go against Bible principles instilled in me? Yes. Judge me in return while you answer this: Why be in leadership for such a selfish reason?

Real leaders speak up for the little people. They shine light where darkness can lead to burnout and toxicity if left in the hands of the wrong person. If you do not think, *I wish to help people who cannot help themselves and push people to be their best versions*, you need to rethink your choice. Do not even think about applying because you will only be able to keep up the charade for so long. Your people will see through you eventually. Once trust is gone, you do not get it back. Once there's negative chatter about you, it's difficult to change the narrative.

I am not writing from a high horse. I have forced myself to consider all these questions and sentiments as well. During my reflections, it became even more important for my real-life talents to translate to my work. Climbing the ladder, I kept finding every role boring after nine to twelve months. I was not being stimulated, and I had to learn that this is my responsibility, not my employer's. Though I never let it show performance-wise, always a type-A overachiever, I found it hard to stay energized and engaged, even when given full autonomy to solve a problem and asked minimal questions along the way.

There was also the fact that I was always the "only" in the room. I would be the "only" Black person on the team. I would be the "only" woman. I would be the "only" Black woman. I would be the "only" person in my age group or generation. I would be the "only" person without children. I would be the "only" optimistic person looking for solutions instead of making complaints. I have even been the "only" hungry one in a room filled with complacent individuals who gave the bare minimum.

No matter which "only" I identified with, it was a difficult task to be my authentic self and be taken seriously. Too bubbly? I am being fake. Too forthcoming? I am being too pushy. Too "let's get it done now"? I am doing too much. Too "how can I improve"? I am doing just fine, but I am being rejected every time I reach for more. Too "I disagree"? I am angry.

Being a Black person in corporate is one of the most unnatural experiences. Hopefully you do not take this the wrong way. If you are Black, born in the United States, it is likely that your ancestors were slaves, and by default you are naturally affected by Willie Lynch syndrome (worth a Google). (A gentle reminder for you: your ancestors built this country. Nothing that exists today would have been possible if it was not for the hard work, blood, sweat, tears, pain, sorrow, and physical and mental calluses of those who came before us.)

Why am I saying this? When you know where you come from, you stand taller, stronger, with your head up, shoulders back, and chest out. Knowing your people built something from nothing should inspire you to want to do the same. Knowing your bloodline carries some of the hardest-working and talented genes on this planet should give you the push to go for the gold, better yet the platinum. They may have built it, but we are here now, and it is up to us to maintain it and make innovations.

Some believe this to be the duty of God or Jesus Christ. However, "Faith without works is dead" means that if you do not act, how can you expect your blessings to appear? You must work for the change you wish to experience. What if it was meant for you to contribute to a larger picture? How would you know if you never looked up from the ground? Why are you even looking at the ground? Is it because "they" told you to? Who even are "they"?

Regardless of who you identify as your "they," you would do well to hold your head high. Black people have consistently thrived in times of adversity. We do not easily crumble and often outperform those around us. You could say some of us eat excellence for breakfast.

It is for this reason again that I ask you to consider your intentions for leadership. If it is not to be excellent for the betterment of your people, maybe it is not the goal for you. There are plenty of things to do! There will always be a job to do (until or unless robots and AI take over). If anything, the need for authenticity in leadership is so high because how else are we supposed to protect our people from losing their jobs in the future? How do we stand out? Who is to say any kind of customer service role will not be transformed into a chatbot? Artificial intelligence is changing the world, getting stronger, more intelligent, growing every day. It is only a matter of time, which means what you do right now is what matters most.

Something else that matters to me, aside from how my talents show up at work, is how my personality translates to my work. Call me crazy for mainly being in customer service roles but absolutely hating customer service. Like I said, we all have bills, and we all know what sacrifice looks and feels like. But as someone who was raised in an abusive environment, I am just mentally in a place where I cannot and will not handle or tolerate anyone speaking disrespectfully to me. I am not your servant. Here's a perfect example, if you work claims: I wish people would not bring up the fact that their premium pays everyone's salary. It reeks of a nasty superiority complex.

I have already experienced a lesser-than treatment growing up. So when you are forced to endure venom spewed in your direction on a daily basis, for a lengthy time, your tolerance for mistreatment does not exist. I do not and will never believe someone should be subject to abuse for any reason, even a paycheck. Kudos to the companies that specify in their policy that if a person experiences a verbally abusive customer, after three attempts to ask the customer to speak in a professional way, you are allowed to hang up on them.

Those are some of my favorite escalations to handle. I love hearing a voicemail about how one of my best people treated someone "horribly." My first reaction is not *What did my employee do?* It is *What did the customer do, and what is their issue?* That might seem backward, but I find it better than the common approach, pointing the finger at the employee. Why do that when you can reassure your employee that you have their back no matter what, to gain their trust so you can really get down to the root of the complaint? You might find this kind of approach not only gains you trust with your employees but respect as well.

When your team does not feel attacked after they make a mistake, you are fostering a safe learning environment. You can ask the important questions without being met with defensiveness. Once they are on the defensive, you are not far from shutting the door to communication. If the door was previously shut, you may notice it begin to crack open, allowing you to gently slip through with the right question and approach. I have always left things open for people to make mistakes. Maybe they did lose it because a customer pushed them to the point of frustration. We are all only human. I do not ever hold it against them. Depending on the situation, I will admit to doing the same thing during my time on the phones and remind them where we need to be instead.

When I was on the phone every day, I kept true to the person I was talking to, meaning I one-hundred-percent matched their energy. If they were short, I was short (but not unprofessional) because clearly they were in a rush and their time was precious. If they were kind, I made sure they received niceties in return. If they were nasty and aggressive, they received my three warnings, and I was unafraid to use the hang-up button. With my head held high, I would tell my manager immediately and fear no consequence.

Now, being the manager means getting both sides of the story. I always get on my employee's side first. Review their documentation. Then, when I call the customer, I allow their side to be shared. I ask penetrating questions to both people involved. Some will say, "You're not supposed to question the customer." I strongly disagree and view this as a killer and contributor to employee retention to always side with the customer.

If the customer has a problem they want solved, how else are you supposed to get to the resolution without asking the right questions? If big businesses would stop putting the dollar over their own people, it would make for great internal improvements. I make it a point—especially if they take the same tone they took with my employee—to let customers know this is not an environment in which we tolerate verbally abrasive behavior from anyone, and I will hang up on them too if it comes to it. They may have been wronged, but the folks answering the phone (most of the time) did not cause this problem, so why should they be subjected to the residual rage just for doing their job?

I admire the resilience of those on the front lines, any front lines. When you think about it, the person answering the phone is the first line of defense, contributing to profitability, customer retention, and innovation. Working in insurance, those three things are highly necessary. Without customers, no one gets paid. Without new ideas to make the external or internal customer experience better, you will have a hard time keeping up with competition. It is not just about who has the best coverage; it is about how people are made to feel when they ask for help in times of stress and crisis.

Being the first person to answer the phone when a person is distressed requires a certain mental fortitude. The strength they carry is immeasurable. The level of humility is one to note. There are more people than not who genuinely care about customers receiving the best outcome and who really enjoy working in customer service. The impact they make is notable, and senior leaders would improve their teams' success if there were that kind of care internally. You cannot expect employees to take care of customers if employees are not taken care of as well.

I admire leaders who break the mold and stand up for those who are ignored and use their powers for the sake of everyone, not just themselves. I admire leaders whose personalities sincerely want to help the greater picture. You are open and kind. You do not shy away from work or pass off your work, not to be confused with delegation. There is nothing wrong with delegation. A good leader tells the team how to make things better; a great leader models the example and gets down in the trenches alongside their team to push for it.

I wish to be a leader who is unafraid to advocate for the right move to be made in any given situation. I wish for cross-team collaborations. I want real connection for real cohesiveness. Integrity leads the way. Having pride in your work will get you far and models for others to have pride in their work too. There is also something to be said about maintaining a healthy balance of execution and procrastination. Proactivity is the name of the game. Staying ahead so your team is never behind is part of my philosophy and how I allow my authenticity to shine. It can be for you also.

Did I have to adjust to fit in? Is code-switching still a thing? Was there a sacrifice of my personal time to get where I am? Was I willing to change my physical presentation to fit the role? The answer to each of these questions is yes. I did have to adjust, but not in the way you would think. It was a necessary adjustment (more on this later). Code-switching is still a thing no matter what people believe. For me, naturally, like every other Black person, I had to be two steps ahead to have an eyelash batted in my direction. And in my reality, the way I grew up, I always had to dress up.

What kind of power can dressing well translate into the work world? Everything. The dress code standards held by employers have declined year after year, especially since COVID-19. If you work from home, you are probably not dressed half the time. I will admit I am not, but only the bottom half no one sees is usually in sweatpants.

My top half is always appropriate and normally set with pearls, to the point where, if I am not wearing them, certain members of my team will read this as a sign to check on me, which is the funniest yet sweetest thing. How many of you can say your employee-employer relationship is so strong that employees know when you are off or something is wrong, not because of what you said or how you said it but how you are dressed for the day?

There are a lot of people who do not care about management, how managers feel, or what they think, believing they are merely here to get a check. It is literally the best feeling in the world to have employees who see me as a human being and allow *me* space to make mistakes, be ill, have emergencies, etc. "Allow" may not be the word a lot of us want to use, but I use it without shame. I love the grace my team *allows* me. It is good to feel seen and heard, not an enemy but their ally and partner. It makes difficult conversations much smoother.

What about health-wise? Do you take care of yourself? Are you modeling how your team should be considering their mental and physical health? The caregiver and nurturer in me is constantly talking about mental health, encouraging the use of the free therapy offered, discussing my own battles with anxiety, depression, and post-traumatic stress disorder. I show my weaknesses because being transparent makes the team strong. Sometimes, the leader is going to mess up. Sometimes, the leader is going to make a mistake. The leader will not always be right. The leader is not always going to have a good day. The sooner leaders sit with this and allow themselves to be vulnerable, the better off we will all be in the end. How we process our feelings and internal conflicts is vital for the survival of our teams and organizations.

I use a feelings wheel at every opportunity. Whether it is a one-on-one or a group huddle, we start with where everyone is mentally for the day. It helps in processing emotions so we can game-plan, compartmentalize, and be able to push through and complete a task. Or, if they only need an ear, they have both of mine for the time.

Not knowing where your team stands can be to your detriment. Do what you can to get your people to think about how they are doing internally, whether they express it to you right away or not. People need to be able to express themselves freely.

How else will you get to know your people? How else will you know what makes them tick? How are you going to build a long-lasting relationship? How will you show them you can adapt and provide a personable experience versus a cookie-cutter one-size-fits-all for your employees? How will you get someone to listen to you when the trust is not fully there? If you do not know what is important to your employee, how will you encourage them to fulfill tasks or receive and apply your feedback? Why is it important to take an interest in their personal life, interests, hobbies, or whatever is important to them?

You will only find these answers if you truly care. If you do not, you are in leadership for the wrong reasons. How do you expect your employees to show passion when this is something you personally lack? Talk about what you do outside of work. Small talk is sometimes the best talk; it allows you to peek into what they care about so you can find your way in later. Take nothing your employees say for granted. You never know what recollection could save a conversation.

Everything as a leader needs to be about strategy, communication, and results, in addition to the big picture. Many will disagree with what I am about to say next, and that's okay! I believe the "big picture" in customer service is not the product; it's the people providing the service. Make sure your people always have what they need. As the leader, you must be emotionally intelligent, adaptable, flexible, understanding, compassionate, and able to compromise. Working for someone else is difficult. Why make anyone's experience worse? What result will it bring?

If you are in leadership, there is always a mission statement. Does your leadership style and the way you carry your team reflect your company's values, vision, and direction? Do your personal values align with the company? Hopefully, you asked this before you signed off on your offer letter. Taking a leadership role at a company whose values do not align with yours is irresponsible.

There are so many people who are overlooked within the Black community, the AAPI (Asian American and Pacific Islander) community, and the Hispanic community, suffering the slap of watching someone unqualified transition into a leadership role for which they were in competition. It was a slap and a gut punch the time I was overlooked for a manager position for a role I was crushing. Instead, they relocated someone, strategically placed their seat next to mine, and made me their unofficial go-to because I absolutely fielded a ton of questions to help them whenever they needed me. I was used to make someone else look better than they were. This made me think, *If you don't know the role, why are you even here?*

Really, this is the question for us all as we reflect on our intentions for being in leadership roles or roles of influence.

So, why are you here?

What is a self-help business leadership book without a little reflection, right? Are you meant to lead in title and/or in action? What does authentic leadership mean to you?

HOW TO SECURE YOUR AUTHENTICITY INSURANCE
WITH *Intention*

Understand who you are by identifying your why so you
may confirm your direction.

*How can you lead yourself or anyone else if you do not
know where you came from and where you are going?*

Chapter Two

Passion

Time to dig into your childhood again. We will be doing this a lot, so no turning back now. Be brave. You are already here. Thinking about one's childhood can be a trigger. Remember to be gentle with yourself. Hopefully, you had the opportunity as a child to discover what you love most in the whole world. If you did not have this chance, please receive my sincerest apologies. On the bright side, finding your passion as an adult means there are no restrictions to your explorations and adventures. There is no one to tell you no. You are in control of how far you want to go. And I strongly urge you to try right now. It is your time.

What is passion? Per Google, passion is a "strong and barely controllable emotion"; "a state or outburst of strong emotion"; "an intense desire or enthusiasm for something"; and/or "a thing arousing enthusiasm."

Have you ever had an outlet, hobby, or interest that allowed you to be you or discover a different side of you? Have you ever been so passionate about something it kept you up at night? Was there a time where you were your most carefree self? What was the setting? Were you running a ball down a field? Were you mastering the verbal tango of debate club? Was your passion in science, creating new innovations to revolutionize some aspect of our lives? Or were you like me, and your passion, your outlet, was on stage?

In recent times, I have come to realize my real passion was in front of me the entire time. It all started when I was about five or six. I remember my mother putting me in private violin classes. I took private lessons for a short time before the second grade. By the end of the hour-long classes, I was in a performance with the other students. I was too young to remember anything else, other than my late grandmother being in the audience, close to the front, clapping for me, supporting me as she did until her end in 2015. This was the grandmother whose nickname, "Lee," I aim to carry with the highest dignity and pride because I never met a more beautiful person. I would give anything to be a quarter of the woman she was to everyone. She had hands-down the best funeral turnout I have ever seen. Weird thing to brag about, I know. There were a *lot* of people she touched, and they all lined up to pack the Highlandtown Jehovah's Witness Kingdom Hall parking lot when it was time to pay respects. Cars lined the driveway into the streets of Highland Avenue in Baltimore City, and there was nearly only standing room left inside.

It was not just the violin lessons, though. As Jehovah's Witnesses, my mother enrolled me in their Theocratic Ministry School. It was basically a mini university for anyone who wanted to develop their public speaking skills to communicate their message when going door-to-door. Yes, pretty much every Witness who has knocked on your door has been "trained" on how to approach you. Every month or every other month, depending on the size of your congregation, you would receive an assignment for which you researched (sometimes given the source, sometimes not) and prepared talking points. For men, you would get five minutes to educate your audience on your given topic via an oratory speech. For women, the requirements were the same, with the slight difference of delivery. You were assigned a partner for whom you had to script a dialogue instead of a speech. Women were not allowed to speak on stage alone.

It took me until writing this to realize where my passions lie. In a way, I almost feel silly that I never recognized the gifts my family gave to me early in life. Maybe the packaging and follow through as I grew older caused me to disassociate myself, but I am abundantly grateful to have been blessed and exposed to being a writer and performer. Between the private music lessons, research, writing, and stage work, all by ten, I wish I would have had the confidence and support to name myself a musician, writer, and actor.

Here we are, almost twenty years later. I am not shy about it now. And this work I am encouraging you to do on yourself, I am doing right alongside you. I am trying to find my way back to the childhood joys I once knew in an organic way. For a while, I was blocked. At the beginning, I blamed everyone. As time went on, I realized it was *me*. I was blocking me.

After talking to almost seven therapists, being halfway through a 365-day journal, having a hell of a supportive village and life partner, and tons of self-reflection via inspirational podcasts and motivational self-help books and memoirs, I realized I was in my way. Circling back to the supportive partner who always said, since the day I told him I was an artist, "Just do it because you are the only one holding you back," he was right.

Much like the feelings wheel I use, I had to start at the same place. I had to understand why music caused me so much pain when it was my first true love. I had to understand why writing down my thoughts caused me so much angst to find my words. I had to understand why I was so afraid of exploring my passions and how I got to a mindset of deep survival mode.

I would like to preface any future storytelling with the following disclaimer: This book is in no way to bash or disrespect anyone. No one in my past, present, or future. This is just a recollection of my experiences as I remember them and should not warrant any negative actions or disparagement of anyone. This is just a story. My story.

Survival mode began at ten years old for me. Young, right? Why? My parents divorced when I was a baby. I do not remember a time when they were ever together. Sometimes I question why I was born because they were not happy together before I was born, so how or why conceive? Again, not ungrateful, just questions.

I lived with my mom until I was ten years old. Around five or six, I remember she married my pops. We moved to Connecticut because he had a house there. He came with a daughter and a son, just like my mom. It seemed like the perfect fit. The house was over 100 years old. It was big and yellow, one of those multifamily homes with a few bedroom units with separate entrances on each floor. We had a driveway and a huge backyard. We lived in a mainly Hispanic neighborhood, with my elementary school right up the street and a bodega on the corner where we would get snacks after school.

The great memories I had there have only begun to resurface in recent years. I am so glad they are back! The blend of the two families worked out well. I was the youngest. In our house, it was my older (half) brother and my oldest (step) brother. We would see my older (step) sister every other weekend since she lived with her mother. We went to the movies together. We went out to eat as a family after Sunday meetings. Sometimes friends from the congregation would join us. We went in service together. We had game nights. My favorite part? We traveled! Note: I have always had motion sickness or vertigo, and not every road trip was a fun adventure for me. However, I *loved* that our family trips were peaceful and fun . . . unless I said something an eight-year-old should not have said, which usually landed my mom's ring finger across my face, much deserved. I will never forget our first family trip to South Carolina. The fifteen-hour drive there and back, all piled into our Nissan Armada with a mini-TV plugged into a cigarette lighter so we could play movies, will always be a core memory for me.

Something I also remember was having friends freely. I had an actual childhood best friend who I will never forget. She was one of three people with the name Imani or Amani who passed through my childhood. We went in service together. We had sleepovers. We loved the same music. I am pretty sure we tried to have a girl group of sorts. And she had a little sister who I adored, and the three of us were the perfect balance. Even when I lived with my father, every school break I came to visit, we always made it a point to connect. She invited me to her high school graduation, I invited her to mine, and she drove across state lines to come see me cross the stage. When it was her turn, it was a most celebratory time. At mine, I got the first taste of mental health issues before I could recognize what was happening to me. It hit me like a ton of bricks.

Aside from me bombing my graduation song in front of hundreds of people, my high school graduation day was wonderful. It was the first day in my entire life where I felt like the attention was fully on me. Keep in mind, Jehovah's Witnesses do not celebrate holidays or birthdays. Once you count those out, you kind of cut out any room for someone to think anything is truly about them. I guess that is by design. They did, however, celebrate weddings, anniversaries, graduations, and retirements, usually in very modest ways. So finally, here was one day, the first day ever where I was being celebrated in this way. Had we gone out to eat to celebrate before? Yes, of course. This was different. One of my great-aunts offered her home as the venue for my graduation party. I would have a midmorning party and head to my graduation in the afternoon.

My mom's first cousins gathered around me, helping me get dressed and watching while I had my makeup done by my stepmother's best friend. My stepmother, nowhere to be found, along with her children. In fact, my stepmother had not spoken to me the entire month prior to my graduation because she was upset she could not go to the actual graduation. Never mind the fact that she went to more senior celebratory activities than both of my real parents. I feel bad neither of her children got to walk the stage, but that was and is not my problem or fault. Plus, I just did not have enough tickets. My pops had no problem sitting it out, and he drove across state lines and put up for the party. The only person who showed from my father's side was him, my grandma Lee, and possibly my uncle and a cousin, maybe both. That part is a little foggy. I had six tickets, so this meant my bio parents (two), my grandmothers (two), my pops' daughter/my older sister, and my best friend were it.

I wore a white lace spaghetti strap dress. My mom picked it out. It took me years to donate it. She thought it would be tasteful and elegant. And she was right. I was graduating in the top 5 percent of my class, with honors and a finance certification, meaning I could've run my own business straight out of high school if I had known my superpower or understood my purpose at the time.

Yet by the end of my graduation night, there was this immensely thick looming darkness hovering over me and consuming my spirit. On the way from Towson University, where the graduation was held, I was suddenly overcome by such an unknown and deep sadness. I could not cry. I could not scream. I could not focus. I could not tell you what I wanted to do or what I was thinking. Internally, I just felt like being in bed. I did not want to be outside. I did not want to be around people. Only now do I know I was dreading the facts: Not only was high school over, but a full-time job was a *must*. Otherwise, I would be stuck in that house forever. I would have no freedom. I would have zero say in my own life choices. I would never be able to truly be in a safe place living under that roof. If I could articulate an apology to my friend who traveled all that way to be there for me, I would say I am so sorry for ruining what should have been an amazing night on the town, celebrating and making a core memory together. I am sorry she wasted the trip for it to end on such a melancholy note. Instead of being able to compartmentalize like an adult and hold those feelings to myself until after she drove home with my mother, I allowed them to ruin the last time we ever had together. There was no argument. There was no fuss. It was literally just a shift that left silence between us for the night. I imagine it would have been a wonderful time had I been able to be present in that moment. Once real life began, it was over.

I think I felt like things were "over" long before this graduation though, and I just never wanted it to be the truth. In my own childish not-knowing-any-better "oh shiny new thing" kind of way, when my father got married a few years after my mom remarried, I asked if I could move in with him and his new family. He said yes, and my mother, not knowing how much it broke her heart, said yes too. After my fifth-grade graduation, my father drove me back home with him. I had no idea what was in store for me, and I never expected what was on the horizon.

Upon first moving in, the rooms had not been fully figured out. I remember sharing with another (new) older stepsister for a little. I remember the largest bedroom went to "the boys," while the intent was still on my older (half) brother staying connected and sharing with my (new) younger stepbrother. My father and his wife had a master suite in the basement, so they had a whole area blocked off to have a wall put up in the basement. Sound chaotic? It was. And that was just the living arrangements.

Once I was settled, I could not tell my stepmother's intentions. However, her impact was heavy when she drove a wedge between us and what little family we had by insinuating a coed sleepover between cousins who grew up together like brothers and sisters would result in some kind of freak orgy. But the accusation was one of the things that made my older brother never want to come back. It was certainly top three on my list of terrible things she said out of her mouth. My brother did in fact never come back to visit after the first year of me living there, ever. I only saw him when I visited my mom.

When it came to socializing, long story short, I had zero friends my own age. I was the oldest of all the children in the congregation, and then there was a six-year gap between me and my stepsister. I was always hanging out with someone who was on average twenty years older than me. There were benefits. Not everything was wrong with being around grown adults with cars, full-time employment, and no kids of their own who liked me. The adults thought I was a "good young person." Most of the time, someone was willing to treat me to the McDonald's next door to the Kingdom Hall.

I was not allowed to be friends with kids from school outside of the school and was normally discouraged from getting too close while in classes. And within the religion, by the time I made friends my own age, the cliques within the different congregations around Baltimore had already been established, so it was hard to find a place. Without friends or any loyal allies, it seemed I was a lost cause in a losing war, happening in my household nearly every day. Unlike the memories I have of my mom's house, I am not exaggerating when I say I do not have many good memories of living with my father. It was in this environment that my mental health issues manifested in forms of anxiety, depression, harmful and suicidal thoughts, and eventually post-traumatic stress disorder.

There is nothing like being in survival mode mentally when you are in survival mode physically too. It got low at times. I had panic attacks in front of my classmates and had to go to the nurse's office for hours to recover. There were points during high school where I did not want to be alive. I did not feel safe anywhere. People in the congregation were seeing the dysfunction of my household, yet no one would dare speak up or attempt to offer even a brief safe haven or respite. Though I wanted to be done with it all, I never tried anything out of fear of judgment. Thank goodness I did not follow through. I think I can safely say this specific demon is gone now.

Since we are speaking about demons, for the purpose of this book, I will center around three things I discovered while unrooting the weeds growing inside me. To return to my passions and authenticate myself to be an inspiring leader, I had to go deep. Everyone has demons. No matter how close to perfect you may think your life is, there is not one of us who is without error.

For a very long time, my demons have been a body complex, from being body-shamed, neglected as a child, and abused mentally, emotionally, and physically. With these things visible to enough people in the congregation, people's silence always baffled me. It was only after I stopped coming to meetings after my grandma Lee passed away that I heard so many people knew about how problematic things were for me. How disappointing "see something, say something" did not apply.

The body-shaming started on arrival. I was a darker complexion than I am now and still very much looked like my father, not that he is not a handsome man. I would be lying, though, if I did not admit I sang to the mountain top when my mom's face decided to show up as I began high school. Hallelujah! It was a *long* road before then. Arriving for middle school to start in a few months, I remember the talks of getting me to slim down. My father believed it was baby fat, rightfully so, and believed I would grow out of it. We were a stepfamily, and it was obvious because none of us looked alike, but I guess I looked too different. Somehow, his fight over the matter waned and waned over time.

My father did his best. He worked nights so he could be there when I went to school and came home from school. Because of his schedule, most of our relationship was spent in my grandma Lee's Lincoln Town Car, with the baby-blue paint job and blue leather seats. While he was at work, I never knew what to expect from his wife. She had a problem with my father taking me to school. Then it was a problem when I got a part-time job in high school and he drove me. She seemed to hate any alone time we had together and even accused me of wanting to be his wife. I always thought a little girl's first love was supposed to be her dad.

Therein lies the root of the evil. It was not until later that I found out my stepmother never had a dad. She did not know hers until she was an adult. We were not brought around him too often, and when we were, he seemed like he was a lot to handle, respectfully. This was probably one of many reasons she ended up pregnant at eighteen by a young man who also did not want to be a father. History has a way of repeating itself.

By default, she was my guardian in his absence. It was not until I turned seventeen that I realized she never actually wanted this duty. She made sure I felt like an outcast, and her two kids backed her up like henchmen supporting their evil villain boss. It was a losing game. With my stepmother not having a relationship growing up with her father, and then her daughter experiencing the exact same existence, by default it meant they had their hearts removed so early on that all they had was each other, and they only knew how to protect themselves. My relationship with my father appeared to be a subconscious threat to them somehow. I understand now that the sight of me and my father was so unfathomable, and they could not make a place for what they could not understand.

So, if my stepmother said I looked fat, all I heard were snide remarks or snickering from my siblings. I was teased and made fun of for how clothes fit me. After a point, she would buy clothes that were way too big for me. Oh buddy, did that leave a mark. It is so funny now to think that my father would give her money to spend on me, and she would spend as little as possible and keep the rest for herself. I wish women would stop this practice. If a man gives you money for the children, use it all on them unless he says "get something for you too." To add insult to injury, not only were the clothes the wrong size, but a lot of them were also straight-up ugly and boyish. To try to give you the measure of how much this affected me, I did not wear the correct size shoes until 2022 and did not believe I had the right body for skinny jeans, being 125 pounds and five-one (taller than her!). I had no idea what her problem was at all. Was she trying to humiliate me? Was it my dignity she was after? Was her personal self-esteem so low that she had to crush the confidence my parents gave me before she arrived on the scene?

It was not just the clothes. It was the food too. She heavily tracked my food intake. It did not help that there was never any food in the house. We will get to the "why" of this soon enough. This is no exaggeration. We had no food readily available. I am all for teaching your kids the responsibility of cooking and taking care of yourself. I am even here for a minimalist lifestyle like the one I currently live, spending around $100 per week on groceries. However, this was straight-up negligence. When there was food, I always ate more than I probably should have, which contributes to the hint of an eating disorder I have never been diagnosed with because of my present-day relationship with food. Could you blame me? I never knew where my next meal was coming from. My mom would quite literally have to call my school's cafeteria to add money to my lunch account. She always paid enough for me to have two breakfasts and two lunches. This saved me from having to worry about eating when I went home.

I remember going to be with an (adult) "friend" when I was eleven, maybe twelve. I saw a text message from her to the friend that said not to feed me if I say I am hungry. I did not eat before I went there. Did the friend know? I always wondered if the friend would have listened if they knew I really was hungry. I swear this woman was trying to starve me. I could not believe it. And I still do not understand it. I guess it is not for me to understand. I would never do something like this as a parent. Add heavy exercise to the list, and we have the roots to understand the body-shaming and abuse, which lasted until I moved out, much against my father's wishes. Exercise video after exercise video. She would even bring me to her friends' houses to exercise with them. It was a whole thing. She tried to pretend like she cared, but she was just embarrassed that I was a prepubescent, overweight child, and she did not have the patience to let nature do its work. Once my mom's face started to show up on me and I started to thin out on my own, she had less and less to say, which was not any better. Then came the envy and jealousy. Her children were quite problematic in school, and now I looked like my mother, who was more attractive than her and successful at school. Sorry, not sorry. I know my mama is smart and fine. And you can't tell me otherwise. I am blessed to be her only daughter and to have her face, literally.

I was unacceptable ugly, then unacceptable pretty. It added to the misery of not having anyone support me in my endeavors as I got older. My head still spins sometimes at the thought. Because of this, I held onto music with a tight grip since I was not allowed to play sports, a common outlet and skill builder for teenagers. Every music class I could enroll in, I did. I played violin from second grade to eighth grade, making it to first chair. I started choir in eighth grade. This was also the first year I had dual music classes. It was so perfect. Once I made it to high school, I was in choir and piano. I only did piano for one year and was in choir for all four. There were winter concerts, spring concerts, farewells, graduations, homecomings, county and state competitions, and other events where choir had the opportunity to sing, or I had the opportunity to sing solo. I remember a few off-campus trips, one going to White Marsh Mall to sing in front of Macy's. I especially remember singing solo in a competition where I qualified to perform at state level, and it ended up being a big deal because no one from our school had made it in years.

There were also a few plays. One of note, I was the understudy to my still best friend who earned the role of Annie. Yet, I was never allowed to stay after school too long, if at all. I was never allowed to hang out or make friends with others who shared my craft. I was barely allowed to go to the concerts, which counted as part of my grade for the class. Oh, and do not let the concert fall on a night we were supposed to be at the Kingdom Hall; then we really had problems. I still recall how my separate second high school graduation, where I received my finance certification, fell on a Tuesday, the uproar it caused about whether we would go to see me *graduate*. Ugh, it made me sick!

What I can admit is that my father's wife introduced me to Motown. Without her exposing me to the oldies but goodies, I would not have such an eclectic and expansive taste in music. I like a little bit of everything because I was exposed to a little bit of everything. I will give her credit for this and this only. Hats off to her for doing one thing right.

But there were so many concerts where I would look out into empty seats. When I would get home later, I would discover they were home and could have been there if they wanted to be present. She prided herself on being a regular pioneer (which means she had to track seventy hours of knocking on people's doors per month) over being supportive of me. My father would miss them because of work, even when I told him the date in advance. Work always came first.

I remember *one* night they came, and I forgot which year, but I know it was a winter concert because I dedicated a John Legend song to them for their anniversary, December 16. I do not remember if they were there for the entire thing. I remember seeing them after and forgetting to ask because I was just shocked they were there at all. I believe I had a special message in the program for them and everything, so really my attitude toward it now is *They better have shown up.* How foolish I would have felt if they had left me hanging that night.

Fast-forward to when it was time for me to pursue higher education. There was such a lack of support, another vomit-inducing point. When I asked for my father's information to fill out a FAFSA form for me to get financial aid, he refused, saying I won't qualify for anything because he made too much money. Okay? You make too much money, but there's no food here . . . right. Little did I know, I learned later that if your parent makes too much, then you still are able to get financial assistance via a student loan. I guess, in a way, it was a blessing in disguise since I do not have any student loan debt now (only a crap ton of regular debt). But since the divorce from my mom, everything was about making sure he did not lose again. Another wife, anything. I can see how going to college to pursue my artistic skills could mean he would lose me not just in religion but in life, since he believed the music industry to be full of debauchery. I guess after the Diddy thing, he wasn't fully wrong. However, his unfortunate obsession with not losing lost him probably one of the most important things in his entire life. It seemed he lived in fear more than faith.

Hey, at least he was passionate about something, keeping his family together, even if it didn't turn out how he intended. That is more than a lot of people can say. If I can say anything about the man, my father, underneath it all, was passionate about taking care of his family. The only thing I believe he had wrong was his mindset and how he chose to communicate, and sadly, I inherited his habits. Instead of focusing on not losing, he could have been focusing on winning. Not to sum up all his problems. I cannot find another reason outside of communication because of his traditional mindset, but he eventually faced a second divorce.

Even with all I have described so far, I am proud to say I am my father's daughter. He and I are not dissimilar. Everything really is about family in the end. I realize this is all my father ever meant. All he ever wanted was for his family to come together because he had a troubling example to follow in my grandparents, based on stories I have only heard in recent years. Because of his upbringing, he did not have the tools.

Why would he? The environment he was in, surrounded by traditional and religious circumstances, kept a lot of things under the rug. No one needed to go to therapy when they had Jesus Christ and his Father Jehovah God. No one needed to do anything except trust in Him and believe His Word to be the only true thing and believe the interpretations and understandings of modern man as detailed in all the literature. It is hard to break away from how you were raised, and maybe my father did not know he needed to break away to accomplish his lofty goals. I give him full credit. He stood for doing what you love to do so it never feels like work, and my favorite philosophy of his? If you engage your natural talents or passions, you will always have a job. You could say this is where my entrepreneurial spirit comes from because I can always find or make a dollar out of some cents. Or better yet, make a dollar out of sense.

As a result of my father's example, I find myself wanting to put these ideals into practice. Three of my parents all held down a day or night job and, on the side, practiced a side hustle. My mom had hair. My pops had cars. My father had motorcoach buses. I came from naturally hard workers and leaders, watching how they juggled taking care of family. It is by their leadership examples that I am first inspired to want to be successful in completing the mission of providing for my family. This is what most parents want, to have their kids end up better than they did.

And this is what I intend to make happen. For my family. I was not banged and bruised up early for no reason. I was being prepared for real life happening on top of managing a corporate career. I was being prepared to take on the task of building a legacy, something he talked about frequently. I was being prepared to support my life partner and work together to create something for our future family.

What an endeavor. What a privilege and an honor. I knew, however, I did not want to approach things in the same manner as any of my parents. We all must figure out and do what works for us. We owe no one any explanations if they are not directly assisting in the grand master plan of life. You either support me, or you do not. And it is okay if you do not. I am going to keep going because this mission is not going to complete itself. I must unlock my inner child and do it before it is too late. I must find and exercise my passions, or else the grips of anxiety will never let me go. I must allow happiness its place to dwell freely and uninhibited so my household can have peace to move in sync toward our goals. I must take control of me and the future I want for myself so I can model for my team what it means to overcome and push for what you really want, in our careers and personal lives. We all need to *live* again. Live freely. Live loudly. Live passionately. Why else are we here?

My parents were tradespeople. They worked themselves to the bone and still do. I do not want my parents working forever. I do not want my parents to die in cold hospitals or any other healthcare facility. Most importantly, I do not want them to die without at least seeing a glimpse into the legacy they wanted for me. They will not be around forever.

Time is of the essence. To give them the opportunity to rest and indulge in their passions would be my way of repaying them.

Okay, back to leadership. Is your leadership style affected by how passionately or dispassionately you live your life? Or do you think, what does having passion about something unrelated to work have to do with getting a job done? Why does being happy in real life matter to who you are at work? What is the use of hobbies or personal interests? Can a team or organization survive under a leader who is old-fashioned, close-minded, one-dimensional, lacking drive or passion? Is it too late to explore? How old is too old? How do you know when you need a change? How do you know if you are not already in the process of changing? What is the worst that could happen for a team with a leader who is disconnected from themselves? What does self-connection look like? Where do you start? When will you know you are done?

The reason we took a trip down memory lane is because I wanted you to envision my first battlefield. I lived with my father for nine years. It was a long war. I fought it. I came out on the other side very wounded. I am just grateful to have come out of it. We all have a first battlefield. We all have demons. We all have a starting point. Hopefully, this glimpse into mine gives you the courage to peer into your own. I hope your journey was not as traumatic. It is true that we are not who we are without tests, tribulations, and trials. This makes it very important to identify the moment or situation that made you forget what you were passionate about.

When did your love fade for the thing you could not go a day without? Did you get the chance to discover what the thing was? Think about it. I implore you to connect to your inner child to find your happiness, find your passion, find you. Being an authentic leader and an authentic individual means you know who you are and can clearly articulate and model this for your people. They see and respect what you bring and are willing to follow someone who shows direction.

I was a leader in two different departments. In one role, I was in a call center managing representatives who were taking first notice calls for people who needed to report a loss and status calls for people who were following up on existing claims. In the other role, I was leading adjusters who were responsible for a dedicated caseload. The call center was for personal lines customers, and the team of adjusters handled commercial customers. The environments were very different; however, my approach to each was the same. *Passion for the people.*

Responsible leaders should inspire their teams and motivate them to want to do better, to be the best. This was my way. The first time, it worked very well. The connection between my first team is still there, and I even gained some real-life friendships after moving up.

Insurance may not have been what I wanted to do, but there was no way I was going to underperform. Being Black, if you do not perform, you are only hurting yourself. I also never wanted to know what being fired felt like again. I was undoubtedly terrified, especially the year I thought I was going to be fired because I was given a warning. Upon becoming a leader, there was no way I could ever allow anyone to feel how I felt when I was told I missed two metrics out of an entire scorecard for nine months, yet I was never given any solutions from leadership. It was because of this that the people-first approach became my philosophy.

By this adoption, I gained trust in people who you might have thought I would never be able to work with or help coach to a level of proficiency. I was truly tested in managing adjusters. They were different because of the type of insurance setting and tenure. On my first team, I dealt with brand-new hires, most of which were fresh and green to the insurance industry and/or to the company. This, in part, was why my resolve was so strong to ensure their experience was one of the best. There was no way I could sleep at night if I knew how I treated someone negatively affected their outlook on their work, career, or the company. Not taking things personally is something I admittedly am working on, but this would be something too personal. People remember how you make them feel more than anything.

In dealing with a tenured team, with experience ranging from two to thirty years, I had to realize I was coming into a group of people who had already been made to feel negatively before I came on the scene. I started out in a losing battle. Their minds were already made up about many things, and here I am trying to make things better. The audacity of me. To come in and hold people accountable was probably the biggest problem over my first summer, putting me in survival mode at work. I was called racist, which got me investigated and senior leadership's eyes on me. I was ignored when I asked for certain tasks to be taken care of or things to be done a certain way. I was disrespected in difficult situations.

Was it fun? No. Was it what I needed? Yes. It was the perfect experience to test whether I was built for leadership at all. It was the perfect "do you mean it?" time for reflection because, for a long time, I always said I was not a people person. I am an introvert by nature and an extrovert when necessary or when my passions are on display. Landing this difficult role made me stronger and reinstated my thick skin. It confirmed, at least for me, that I was supposed to be in leadership. Dramatic, sure. Reaffirming, one-hundred-percent.

I thought I could only have one passion. How closed-minded! By sinking into my real-life passions as a woman of the arts, I rediscovered how much people reciprocate the energy you give them. My taking care to connect with myself allowed me to connect with others. When I was younger, I performed on stages, and this opened doors for conversation. As a leader, there is no difference. You are on a stage. Your team and organization are watching what you will do to add to their jobs and work life. Are you making their lives easier, more manageable, or is their day-to-day difficult for no reason? My passion to take care of my people defied odds, and I am proud to have led such wonderful teams despite pretty much being on autopilot (meaning I normally do not hear a peep unless someone has a question or there's an escalation). With teams who grew stronger every day, I find myself answering less questions over time. Their self-confidence, successes over time as a team, and increased comfortability with each other meant they leaned on one another instead of only me.

Through very specific tests, I learned that being myself was the only way to success. Having passion and a vested interest in my people kept time moving swiftly. I was serious about everyone's development, including my own, when I asked for the person who called me a racist to be removed from my team. Truthfully, since it was an anonymous survey, they should not have identified themselves. After they did, it was downhill. I told my manager I literally could not do my job with this person on my team because any time I brought up an idea, it was a fight. The last straw was them arguing with me in front of the team.

At the same time as their removal, I was working on a performance action plan for another employee who literally did no work. The team knew it. I knew it. The leader before me knew it, and later I found out it was partly because the leader was doing the work for them to cover. If you cannot tell how much I am not down for picking up slack in this way, you are not reading me correctly. I was not about to do someone else's work for them. And the team was suffering too because they were dealing with the slack directly, handling overflow calls for angry customers. It makes morale very low when a leader allows people to do whatever they want, and it negatively affects the team.

It was not lost on me that there were favorites. I had an open conversation about this with half of the team. Being new to the department and unit, I observed and did not pass judgment. I still do not. I saw what they were talking about and did what was in my control to make my immediate team a safe space. Maybe they saw it after the peer swap, or maybe they saw it after the teammate who did zero work was no longer with the company. Either way, protect your team and their mentality at all costs.

Also, passion for your people looks like investing in their growth. You may have people who do not want to climb the ladder. Some people like and prefer the front line. Bless their hearts. Once the team was free of the spirit of lackluster in work and change, we could finally get on a cadence. Our huddles had structure, mainly because I could finally focus, and from this stemmed a new structure in our huddles and one-on-ones. Our weekly team huddles begin with everyone going around the room describing themselves via a team-designed feelings wheel. We then give the opportunity for everyone to give positive feedback to each other. If we have a guest speaker from a different function, they present after they see us exchange encouraging words. After any guest speaker, we go into announcements, then discuss the team's overall health, including scorecards, quality results, and best practices. After the team health, we watch a ten-minute or less development-related video on YouTube (found by me or the team) to highlight areas of opportunity in our professional and personal development: time management or even just something motivational to pick up spirits. After the video, we close with personal affirmations.

The structure did not stop there. Our one-on-ones became more meaningful too. The three questions in their OneNote notebook pages, for every one-on-one conversation, would be "What's on your mind," "What's on the agenda," and "What's the plan?" *What's on your mind* is open-ended, and I encourage them to share their feelings from the feelings wheel so I can understand where they are mentally and know how to carry the rest of the conversation. *What's on the agenda* moved us into our work-related conversation, discussing strengths, opportunities, and any problem claims. And *what's the plan* was where we discussed goals and best practices to achieve their stated goals. While the requirement was to meet with your team for one hour a month, I moved to meet biweekly with my folks for one hour (eventually forty-five minutes) because one hour per month, to me, is not enough when you genuinely want to know someone or find the root of what's missing in your team's success.

With this approach, sooner than we knew, we had a flow. Our hard work was paying off. We were landing on recognition lists and being praised for doing great work. We consistently received positive customer feedback that they would forward via email, and we even had customers leave praiseful voicemails versus the normal nastygram message.

Taking the time to bond with your people and getting to know them on a personal level is worth it, much like a parent takes interest in and supports their child's passions and desires. Do not let anyone tell you otherwise. It is worth it, sure, because the work gets done, but think bigger. You are making an impact on someone's life. When you stand for people, they do not forget you. Be genuine and authentic and encourage your people to be better people first and employees second. Their respect for you will grow.

We cannot expect people to just want to come to work and be the "ideal" employee anymore. We must model the ideal employee: flexible, understanding, hungry for growth and development, patient, emotionally intelligent, modest, and, above all, kind and respectful. It is difficult to not be naturally passionate about leading a team when everyone is on the same page with you about the direction the team should be going and everyone is dedicated to the team's mission. We are all working on something completely different from another, and the fact that we all know we are working on something pushes us harder.

Passion begets passion. Passionate leaders make for passionate and inspired employees. Passionate and inspired employees make for high-performance cultures and a well-rounded atmosphere. High-performance culture in safe atmospheres makes for profitability. The math maths.

So, are you counting on you yet?

Write down your biggest passion(s) in life and how you would monetize it (or them) if possible. What would it look like if you worked for yourself and did what you love?
Do not fight it. Just write it. And if it becomes real, excellent.

HOW TO SECURE YOUR AUTHENTICITY INSURANCE
WITH *Passion*

Dig deep to (re)discover your joy in your natural talents
to find inner alignment.

*If you are not doing what you love, what are you doing
with your life?*

Chapter Three

Transparency

Wouldn't we all prefer to know the truth from the start? Or is there a part of you that does not mind a little merry-go-round? Do surprises bother you? If your life was upended in an instant, how would you rebound? Would you want to know everything right away in the heat of change, or would you want to be paced through it? How would you feel if your questions could not be answered?

Personally, I would rather know what's coming before it gets here. Do not waste your time trying to concoct a story behind bad news to build up to it. Do not lie or hold onto it until the "right time." Rip the Band-Aid off. Give it to me straight. This mentality for me began at home, living under weary conditions and becoming desensitized. And the belief was strengthened as I tried to progress in my career by putting my name in the hat for higher grade level adjuster and manager roles—and I received rejection after rejection.

Solution-less feedback is a waste of everybody's time, just an FYI. Telling someone what they did wrong without telling them how to fix it is an example. Rejecting someone without telling them why is also an example because you are not giving the person the opportunity to understand what they could have done differently or their missing qualifications for them to go get the experience you seek. There is always someone out there who is better than us. The competition is rough out here, especially if you are trying to get by on pure talent, hard work, and experience, without an actual degree. Having a finance certification has not opened any doors, and if I am being real with myself, if I had to look at spreadsheets all day, I do not know what I would do.

In the various roles I have held around claims, to be fair, I have never really known what to do with myself. At times, the leaders around me did not seem to know what to do with me either. No matter what role, somehow, I found myself veering back to my writing skills. I would create resource guides, communication templates, PowerPoints, you name it, to help my team stay on top. And once I started using Canva for work, things really got interesting. I liked to be the best and wanted others around me to be the best too. We all did things differently, but the foundation of claims is the same no matter what kind of claim.

I guess you could say I always did more than just my job description, always trying to prove I was capable of more. Five years of being overlooked was enough for me. Never had I imagined I would be an adjuster for so long. I was exhausted and burned out after my third year. I was considered multiple times for leadership roles. The feedback I received? "If I was hiring for a permanent manager role, you would be it." It took me talking to various mentors to break down the meaning behind this rejection, to understand that the person hiring thought I'd require more time to settle into the role than someone who could hit the ground running. *Tsk tsk.* A poor assumption.

Personally, I believe myself to be adaptable, a quick study. It is a shame what biases exist when people do not really get to know you. In the same breath of being told "no" for the position, I was asked for my opinion. Who should get the job instead of me? I did not realize until later the inappropriateness of this conversation. I was trying to look like a good sport and less like a sore loser. I kept my opinion professional. I said the person who gets overlooked should have the opportunity to prove themselves for once. I could never stand someone being treated like the favorite. I will always root for the underdog.

The irony is that I vouched for a White male as the "overlooked" party to another White male whose decision it was to fill the role. I still laugh about it. Full systems have been designed by them to "overlook" people in the Black, Brown, and Asian communities. Corporate is one of those systems.

If you had access to the organizational charts of a lot of major companies, the higher up you go, the less representation of diverse backgrounds exists. So, where I sit, any time someone from an underrepresented demographic obtains a promotion, it is a real celebration. A win for one of us is a win for all of us when the statistics do not work in our favor. Be prepared; anyone believing a smooth vertical-ladder climb exists is in for a hell of a ride. This is proven by the low percentages of BIPOC (Black, Indigenous, and people of color) CEOs that exist within the Fortune 500 list.

There is nothing smooth and sometimes nothing vertical about the corporate ladder climb for people like me. Some folks in my village have had lateral moves. Some have been demoted due to organizational remodel. Every few years, something changes, and you have to roll with it. Because of unexpected and sudden changes, I value being a transparent leader and having transparency from those leading me. In a time where change can be so triggering, telling it like it is earns you the authenticity insurance necessary to lead your teams through tough times.

Transparency is being honest and open with your people. How else do you build trust? The wall between you and them has to come down. The good news is you can control *how* the wall comes down. You can make people feel like they are valued and push them to have confidence in what they do. Obviously, there will be things you should *not* share, like why a teammate is out on leave.

A pivotal piece of information most people want to know is why. Why is the change occurring? Why here and now? Why is my cooperation important to the team or organization?

Some probably fear sharing the "why" because of what doors it might open. If you don't have the answers, maybe you fear your team will lose faith in you. It is, in fact, quite the opposite. You do not have to know everything because you are the leader. People respect you more when you say, "I do not know the answer, but let me find out for you." As long as you follow through with it, you'll never get so much as an eye roll in response.

And trust is a *huge* part of that. Trust issues can stem from dating or home life. I mentioned earlier that a girl's first love is supposed to be her dad. And he was until he broke my heart. Part of the communication issues had to do with his lack of transparency. He kept secrets and was tight-lipped. He sought control via manipulation. And for a while, he had it.

I knew he was a firm believer of "what happens in this house stays in this house." Perhaps this is why no one in the congregation dared to speak about the very blatant things they saw. I do not fault anyone for minding their business. But I will always wonder what would have happened if my father was more transparent about . . . everything.

Much later, I found out one of the reasons why he did not keep food in the house was because he was saving up to buy a motorcoach bus so he could work for himself. Told you, the man had passion. He had hustle. His work ethic was unmatched. At what cost? Instead of sharing his dream in detail, he kept it to himself because of fear. Would we work with him? Would we take it seriously? Either way, the longer the conditions remained, the greater the divide.

I do not know all the ins and outs of my father's relationship with his wife. It was and is none of my business. We had dinner for the first time in maybe five years back in 2023. It was so cringy to listen to him tell me about his marital issues. With how I view things now, it should have been evident from the jump that they were not a fit. Neither were transparent about what they were looking for or their dreams or aspirations. Support was withheld.

I remember how much they were on the phone in the beginning

and how much their conversations eventually lessened. If there was a conversation, it seemed more like an argument lighting up the house. Sometimes during the daylight hours, sometimes in the middle of the night. My stepbrother would try to help. Internally, I would laugh and think, *Have a seat, young man. If I can Sparta-kick you into a dresser and send you flying* [a true event], *imagine what my father will do if you try anything.* There was also part of me that thought it was normal. Why get involved at all? All parents argue, right? Until I entered my current relationship, I never realized how problematic it was to allow your children to hear details about your marriage. It shapes how your children think, learn, problem-solve, and communicate, how open- or closed-minded they will be, and how they view you.

It was the lack of effective communication and damage control after bad things happened that sent our household in the wrong direction. After they finished arguing, he would escape to work and be gone more than half the day. Me? I would be left with her. Bitter. Upset. Emotional. Begrudging. Looking like my father, a reminder for the source of her anger, an easy, defenseless target.

My favorite thing (said sarcastically) she used to do was pick up children from the congregation to babysit and keep overnight. She would buy them clothes and food, take care of them if they were sick, and take them to the movies. What did she do with or for me? Not a thing.

At the beginning, when her daughter still lived with us, I remember she would take me to the nail salon with her, and we would get pedicures together. She did not do it for very long, and when she stopped, it was sudden and abrupt. When I asked her why, she said it was because I was unappreciative. This was my first real example of solution-less feedback. There was no further explanation, nothing for me to self-discover. I was eleven, the only child in the house who did chores and got good grades. Not to mention I would write the dialogue for her Theocratic Ministry School assignments. Yes, I was ghostwriting before I was a teenager for a forty-year-old. What could have been unappreciative about me? Me making you look competent in front of your peers?

Come to find out later, the pressure for her to side with her daughter was very high. Unfortunately, there was a dispute leading to my stepsister cursing at my father and putting her hands on him. With the old-school mentality of my father, these two things meant only one thing: "She got to go/She can't stay here anymore." How upsetting and divided my stepmother must have felt to have to swiftly help her daughter pack all her things in several large, black forty-gallon contractor trash bags, to move her into my stepgrandmother's house ten minutes away. How abandoned my stepsister must have felt, her mother choosing her husband.

I cannot imagine what it must have felt like to not have a father, and then the only person who has ever had your back in life since birth, your mother, having to choose her spouse over you. I cannot imagine my stepsister's feelings of being an outcast or how much pain she must have been in under the circumstances. She and I never had a relationship. And with my stepmother not having her father around or liking her marriage and taking it out on me, this is why we do not have a relationship. As a grown woman, she had the choice to not abuse a defenseless child who was entrusted in her care. She went out of her way to exude kindness to everyone else's children and not me. Was I not deserving of love too?

And this is when communication comes into play. Telling people the truth the first time leads to real, open communication. Communication with your teams should always be open. You are not a tyrant or dictator. Be humble and realize that your team keeps everything running. Without them, you will fall behind. They will be fine without you; you will not be without them.

Fostering a transparency-based environment means your team will be willing to raise concerns about their work, peers, and you. Feedback is a gift whether we want to return-to-sender or not. Feedback from your team is crucial to success. It is how you check the pulse. Where is everybody? How do you measure the next steps?

From your team, you will get the best questions and ideas for continuous improvement opportunities, which ultimately contribute to profitability. Even in claims, each member of the team does their part by ensuring exceptional customer service. Transparency within leadership benefits every industry.

Take the lead in asking questions. I view my team as the real experts. I might steer the ship, but they know every inch better than I ever could, and this is why we win. I probably ask them "why" more than they ask me.

If you are trying to hold your team accountable, you must ask the right questions. Being the leader does not mean your questions have to be complicated. "Why" posed the right way can do the trick. Or a "walk me through how you got here" in a non-accusatory way can be helpful. People respect you more when you ask questions before jumping in to make a change.

Since I inherited a tenured team, my questions and approach were top priority. Initially, I only sprinkled in a little bit of change based on incoming feedback. I wanted to give time for people to settle into the idea of me being the leader. I wanted to observe how they operated. Were they current with their workload? How often were there customer complaints and escalations? And what was the root of the complaints? How did their metrics compare to their peers? When you come in quietly, you can learn a lot in ninety days.

And I did. Combining my observations with questions, I learned one of the major issues boiling within the team was accountability. Accountability for how the team was being led, the work being completed, the outcomes, individual work, the environment. What was the direction of the team? Where was everyone going? Were they all going to be adjusters forever? What was everyone's long game? Had anyone ever been asked this prior to my arrival?

Transparency through accountability is not only about making sure people get the work done the correct way. It is about lighting the path for people to see where they are going, holding people accountable for the outcomes they claim to want. I have had leaders ask me immediately where I want to go on day one of a new role. Soon enough, this became one of my first questions when getting to know my team and a recurring question to help keep folks on track. Where do they want to go? Where do they see themselves? What you believe you see in your employees is no match and completely irrelevant if the person does not see themselves there too. Listening to understand your people's desires and having the wherewithal to hold them accountable to reach their goals will make you stand out as a leader.

A person's career is their own. It is up to them to own it, to harness their energy, to use their powers for good, to compartmentalize and upcycle negativity into positivity to get through the heavy workloads and unexpected changes. A full moon is the catalyst between a steady day and a dumpster fire in claims. Ask anyone. As the leader, their coach, it is your responsibility to hold them accountable to stay on track. Offer guidance and counsel. Your job is to help them accomplish what they set out to do. They will work harder when you believe in them.

With you believing in them, they are bound to make strides. Build up trust by creating the foundation for a healthy relationship and a two-way street for communication that is rarely closed for construction. We must allow people a safe space to express themselves because we cannot be anyone else. Consistency in these areas is necessary for people to feel empowered over time. Once you have a team full of empowered employees, you will find that the sky is the limit.

Transparency can empower employees, depending on how you do it, to understand their role's purpose and give them the opportunity to think bigger for themselves, especially if they see themselves evolving in their career. One way I help my team get the bigger picture is something I mentioned earlier: inviting people from other functions to our team huddles. The guest speaker introduces themselves, talks about their career and their journey, and discusses their team's responsibilities and day-to-day. This facilitates a discussion on how our teams can better operate together to support one another if there is any intersectionality.

We had guest speakers from our immediate surrounding functions, such as underwriting, finance, special investigations, quality assurance, etc., who brought us insight into their world. Each person conducted their presentation with great care. We heard from leaders and individual contributors who did not have direct reports. With each visit, the team grew stronger. Our one-on-ones were venturing into discussions about job-shadowing others in different roles. Finding guest speakers was my way of supplementing networking, recognizing that those working the front lines (in claims) do not often have time to step away from their work. Employee resource group activities are in some ways a joke to front-line folks, primarily because anything taking away from the work contributes to this never-ending cycle of thinking you are behind. And worse, you think you will get in trouble for attending company events designed to help people network and grow. As much as I advocated that one hour per month will not hurt the bottom line, the message still fell on deaf ears. If it does not come from senior or executive leadership, it will never truly be accepted by the front line.

It saddened me when employees were not aware of resource groups. I thought, *Why and how does this happen?* Within onboarding standards, all new employees should be introduced to the employee resource groups. I took charge by putting employee participation on our goals list to attend events and share takeaways with the team.

Getting your people to take ownership of their careers and their time spent at work will strengthen everyone. Working for a global company, the amount of people holding it together is unfathomable. There are departments on top of departments. This was my experience. It seemed as if every time I changed roles, there were more pieces of the puzzle to connect for it all to make sense.

For anyone who has attempted an insurance designation like an associate in claims (AIC) or chartered property and casualty underwriter (CPCU), you are familiar with the term "insurance value chain," used to define what keeps an insurance company running. If you are unfamiliar, the term "insurance value chain" is used to define the various areas contributing to what keeps an insurance company running via different areas offering products or services or supporting the offered products or services.

Insurance obviously has sales, where we have agents offering the product of protection to commercial businesses or to everyday people like you and me. How do people know about the products if not from a salesperson? Well, you need a good marketing department. Marketing takes care of attracting business to keep agents from having to rely on cold-calling or heavy solicitation. Who writes the policy being sold by the agent after it was advertised by marketing? This ball gets passed to underwriting, who is responsible for reviewing applications to ensure the policies are being sold to trustworthy customers who will be able to pay their premiums and have lower and acceptable chances of risk.

Who is there to take care of all the revenue coming in from these functions? Well, moving right along to finance, those who count the money, save the money, invest the money, and ensure the right decisions are made to keep all the funds flowing properly. Who takes care of the internal customers to handle payroll, hiring, company policy violations, and other employee issues? You guessed it. Human resources or talent operations. Who takes care of the external customers calling to utilize their policy? You are in claims territory now. And last but not at all least, who takes care of technical issues? Come on, everyone needs a phenomenal IT department. They are the backbone. When it all falls, IT is tasked to save the day.

But it is easy to get buried in your own work, to not come up for air. If you are a leader and wish to see your people do better, expose them to as many facets of the company as possible. It is not your job to keep things exactly as they are. It is your job to embrace change and help others embrace and want change.

As I talk to my people about their careers, my first question is this: "Do you want to stay in claims?" Is it due to my own jadedness? Yes, but it is still a valid question. How can you know what their goal is if you never ask? How can you know what they want to do or where they want to be or understand their intentions if you never ask?

Speaking with one senior leader, I said, "I hate claims." This was probably not the thing to lead with, and most would have shied away from it. But that is not who I am, and fortunately, I don't believe my authenticity made this leader like me less (at least I don't think). I believe in my head-on approach. I do not want anyone to ever get the wrong idea about where my eye is set. Claims is not where I chose to be but where I want to be until it no longer serves my household.

I cannot tell you how many rejections I received because a hiring manager or recruiter could not connect my skill base to the responsibilities in the job posting. At least now, due to rising standards and angry people, you are more likely to receive feedback. Whether it makes sense is another story. I have also received feedback that did not apply to me, as if it was pulled out of thin air.

The method in which feedback is delivered may also vary. You could get the normal face-to-face conversation with specified feedback. You could receive a generic email sent to all candidates who did not make the cut. And now you could even receive a standard rejection video. Yes, I said video. Fancy stuff, but it's solution-less feedback.

What do we do about it? How do we get employees to believe our transparency? To trust us? To openly say what brings them down and what builds them up? To dream with us? To be accountable? To be empowered to take control of their careers and their lives?

Do not be afraid to be a human. This does not mean to move and speak without discernment. It means just what it means. *Do not be afraid to be a human.* Personally, this has proven very helpful in maintaining my authenticity. People will say your team needs to always see you perfect. This is so far removed from reality. The year is 2025. We do not have to hide who we are anymore.

If our environments are rigid and cold, if there is no growth, if people are quitting left and right, if restlessness exists, if disparity is continuing to harbor a mentally unsafe workplace where talent cannot develop equitably, who is the problem? Who is responsible for fixing it? While we would all hope major issues would be addressed at the head, it does not always work this way. *Be* the example you wish to see. Create the environment you know is necessary.

Start with yourself. If your people do not know who you are, it is because of *you*. The less you share, the more you appear closed. To look like a human, you must be a human. Talk about your real life (without bragging). When breaking out the feelings wheel, take a moment to share where you are with your people, and tell them why! If you are happy, say the reason. If you are uneasy, express the feeling. Your people will see you as being affected and allow more grace to flow freely. I do not suggest disagreeing with the changes outright (depending on your audience). It's important to be in alignment with the company, but sometimes a little rebelliousness has its advantages. Approach with extreme caution. You can express discomfort about something and still be seen as a leader.

As leaders, we do not always have it together. We experience every emotion on the feelings wheel, like anyone else. What is the point of hiding your emotions? Your emotions make you who you are, and how you handle them confirms whether you should be in leadership. If you cannot express, "I feel excited today because our team is being recognized for great work, but I cannot help but feel sad because when I log out, I am overwhelmed at home," then think hard about whether you can be a leader. Can you model an environment in which your employees can prosper?

Being human has earned me respect, trust, support, kindness, and, believe it or not, real friendships. "You are not supposed to be friends with your direct reports," some say. How many of us have heard this? All of us, right? Did the person saying this bring up the definition of "friend" before shoveling out this warning? Probably not.

Look it up right now. There are many definitions. I am not saying be friends on social media or have frequent exchanges outside of work. There is a line of professionalism and decorum to maintain. Plus, be realistic. We spend forty-plus hours per week with our team. Respect that they need their space too, as do you.

A friend is someone on the same side as you. Last I checked, you would make for a terrible leader if you made enemies out of the people who report to you. There is nothing wrong with befriending your people because it is literally to show them you are on the same side.

Who is listening to someone bark orders anymore? You need to adapt to be able to deliver feedback in a graceful and kind way. Avoid "fussing," being argumentative, and being too sharp. No one wants to deal with a smart-ass. That is a surefire way to have a report against you. If you view your people as people and take time to befriend them, you will stand out.

For women, befriending people and controlling our emotions can be a hard tango. But you can and will find a rhythm. You will know when to show your human side. And you will know when to show your "boss" side. If anything, being a woman, connecting with our emotions innately gives us the upper hand. It is the lack of control in our actions, our words, and our own accountability when we do something wrong that creates doubt in others who say things like "women cannot lead." You probably witnessed and heard a lot of these attitudes toward women during the 2024 US presidential election and likely many other arenas where women's competency comes into question. Do not let notions like this deter you. They are only true if we feed it with the very actions proving the point. So let's take back the narrative and make the change.

Women have great success with being authentic because a lot of us don't hide how we really feel about anything. Men are more likely to hide how they feel for fear of judgment and rejection. In regular conversation, you will know when a woman disagrees the millisecond it happens. Verbal words are one thing. I am talking about the body telling on you too via its physical expression. Sure, you said yes. The nerve above your eyebrow that popped out says something else. And an eye twitch is certainly a sign, if not of a vitamin B12 or D deficiency, of an issue at hand. A blank stare is not even safe.

Trust me. I have always had RBF. It means "resting bitch face" if you are unfamiliar, and for me it was part of my defense mechanism growing up when being yelled at for no reason. Ultimately, to me, it was a blank face. I could not cry when I was left alone with my stepmother and her children for fear it would make me look weak and fuel the ridicule. Turns out, what I really ended up doing to myself was mastering RBF, which was quite the opposite of the intent behind the face. I was trying to protect myself back then. Now I make it a point to smile when it makes sense to remind people I am not upset or angry. This is just my face. Sorry we cannot all have perfectly structured model faces that merely exist effortlessly, beautifully, and flawlessly. Some of us have to work for our beauty, said laughingly. If only my eyes smiled all the time. This alone would solve my problems.

Yet again, though, this is not something I am referencing as a weakness. If you discover a weakness or opportunity on your own, give yourself credit for your self-awareness and the fact that you figured it out. We do not all develop and even utilize self-awareness in the same manner. I say this because these are the things making women human too. Acknowledging I have RBF has gotten me nothing but hearty laughs out of some of the most stiff and dry rooms. Truthfully, it is a funny and factual icebreaker.

Being transparent about your emotions is a positive adaptation to your leadership style. Transparency will save you time and energy. Saved time and energy means you can place your focus on more pressing areas, which improves prioritization. Improved prioritization contributes to resources being allocated properly. Properly allocated resources means less waste. Less waste makes for savings. Savings contributes to profitability. More profit means more money if your company promises any kind of annual individual or company performance-based bonus.

There is no other way to break this down. Transparency about who you are as a person is necessary to get people to believe in you and back you. Be transparent about your team's strengths and weaknesses. Why cover up failures when you can teach people how to avoid the mistake again?

Divulge when changes will happen because people may be afraid. Be afraid with them. Be reassuring. Be kind. Talk openly about everyone's feelings and concerns. Be brave by asking for their feedback about you. Be open to receive their feedback because once you offer to hear what they think about you, there is no turning back. You must take it, acknowledge it, and respond appropriately. You cannot be fake about open communication if you expect people to be held accountable or to feel empowered or to see you as a regular person capable of detaching from your title.

This way of thinking might make you nervous. This is okay. This feeling is normal. I have overseen teams with brand-new hires and those with thirty years of experience. Telling the truth even when it hurts only brings teams closer together. I have had the pleasure of assisting in and initiating promotions for several people who have been in a role for less than a year. Being transparent got me the results I needed to ready the person for the next steps.

Adopting transparency into your skill set will add to your authenticity because it will strengthen your ability to connect with peers, direct reports, senior leaders, and people outside of work (transferable skills). You will set the tone for conversations where people will be disarmed because they will believe you are genuine in your intentions and not their enemy. You all share a common goal. You will get there faster and safer with more support. You will arrive at your best because you had others' faith behind you all from you telling it like it is and being brutally honest yet respectful.

So, how clear will you be?

STRENGTHEN YOUR SUPERPOWERS. ACTUALIZE YOUR PURPOSE.

Reflect on how you will organically build trust within
yourself, your peers, and your team.

HOW TO SECURE YOUR AUTHENTICITY INSURANCE
WITH *Transparency*

Be a real human by acknowledging we (you, me,
everyone) will always be human first.

*Do the right thing and tell the truth no matter the
potential outcome.*

Chapter Four

Branding

An oversimplification of branding is how we discover what we want based on how the person, product, or service is presented to the consumer. We want to know if we can trust what we are about to buy and trust the people who made it. Does the brand have the consumer's best interests in mind? Are the products in alignment with personal beliefs, such as no animal testing? Is it of high or low quality? What do reviews say? Does the company display philanthropy?

Branding is not just for businesses or influencers on social media. *You* are a brand. Walking. Talking. Living. Breathing. Working. Sleeping. Exercising. Eating. Dressing. Driving. Everything about you represents you. Every time you leave the house. Every time you interact with a stranger. Every time you have a presentation at work. You represent your brand.

It is based on your actions and words. If someone does not like your brand, you will likely not interact with them. If a person finds your brand respectable and intriguing, you might have the right conversations with the right people at the right time. Remember, nothing happens for no reason. You are in control of you. Everyone is watching you, always. So be good. Be great if you can swing it. No pressure. Not every leader is "great." Some leaders exist to fill space to provide balance. It is not always a "good" balance. So, you will need a strong brand to withstand the tests and challenges. People working with you deserve to know what they are getting.

Being raised and baptized as a Jehovah's Witness, having no exposure to any other religious backgrounds whatsoever, created a severe case of tunnel vision, which kept me from identifying their "brand." Based on what they would portray, I thought getting baptized was the only way of life. The branding was another shiny thing to me as a child. Back then, it was exciting. Getting baptized meant hanging with adults in a more "official" capacity, like leading a Bible study with a total stranger. It also seemed like being baptized was the only way to forgiveness, the only way to be respected in this niche community.

I remember being asked what I wanted and saying I wanted to be baptized. I was asked if I understood what it meant. I said yes. At the time, based on what I did know, it was what I wanted to do. If it meant being closer to my family, then yes, I wanted to do it. If it meant being closer to God, then yes, I wanted to do it. Yet, no one told me I would lose my freedom or individuality.

Seriously, though, the question of whether a nine-year-old understands what they are giving up is insane when you think about it. Based on my experience, I do not think it's responsible to baptize a child under eighteen. They do not know anything about literally anything yet. At any age, people are just trying to figure it all out.

If someone said I could not play sports, I would have said no. If someone told me my opportunities to go to college would be ignored over spiritual endeavors, I would have said no. If someone said I could only associate with people who think the same as me, I would have said no. If someone said I could not explore my passions, I know I disappoint a lot of my family by saying I am sorry but never mind.

If I had known that my dreams would be completely affected, I hate to say I would have rethought the whole thing. I do see the perspective of why certain people view the Witnesses as a cult. When I first dissociated myself in 2016 the year after my grandmother Lee died, I would be offended if anyone said anything like that about the Witnesses. I still kind of am because I do not like anyone disrespecting my family. That's still my family and will always be, even if they never truly or wholly accept who I am. Without them, I would not be who I am or where I am. However, I do understand the perspective better now. I could not see because I was still close to it. Taking a step back changed my entire view.

I did not want to sacrifice myself in the expected way. I did not want to run and hide to prepare for a prophesied hostile turn on religions. I did not want to live like the world could end tomorrow (not in the way you think or how people referencing fun endeavors make this statement). I tell my family how hard I work so I can take care of them. They say, "Aw, that's sweet," and then "if this system of things lasts." As someone who openly admits to managing anxiety, depression, and PTSD, I hope my family understands why I move the way I do.

I cannot and will not live as though I will not be here in fifty years. To me, this is irresponsible. Let the world end. God is going to judge me, right? God knows my heart, right? So then why do I need to tie myself to any structured form of religion? Why is it not okay to be a good person on its own merit? I do not sell, buy, or do drugs. I do not rob the poor. I have never been arrested. I have never committed a crime, not even so much as slipped a small item from the checkout line into my pocket when I thought no one was watching me. I feel icky trying to figure out small white lies, let alone trying to hold it together for big ones.

A lot of the Bible-based principles are in me because they were all I heard. But I disagree with a *lot* of them. For example, the practice among the congregation where anyone dating could never be alone. All dates had to be in groups or have a chaperone. No privacy? With someone I would potentially marry? Nope. I will not marry someone I do not know. And never being alone with someone begs the question, how can you know the person? I know I am not sharing my deepest, darkest secrets around a crowd of people. We'll call it group dating.

And as far as I am concerned, group dating is the perfect cover for anyone who has something to hide from an unsuspecting partner who doesn't know you come with a whole bunch of baggage, perhaps an abusive family pathology or even straight-up serial killer vibes.

Did this happen to my parents? What led to their downfall? Was it a case of not knowing who the other person really was? Did it all go to hell in a handbasket after the wedding and moving in together? Did my parents hide who they were? Or did they lack the proper tools to be married?

I am not one to side with any woman just because we "should." If you are wrong, I am going to tell you. Though I do not have all the facts, I know both of my parents contributed to their relationship not working. As far as I know, Bible principles and, realistically, they both were probably not being transparent with one another about who they were, which prevented them from really getting to know one another.

It is for this reason that I have lived with my partner from the earliest point possible. After all I went through, I needed to know the man was safe. It was not until recent years, through a multitude of breakthroughs, that I realized I never treated him like I believed he was safe, in part due to some of his own personal life decisions that affected me and my own inability to move on from trauma. Thankfully and without spite for the stress-added gray hairs in his beard, he has been one of my greatest protectors.

My first experience of my own poor branding goes all the way back to my baptism. It was just before moving back to Maryland from Connecticut to live with my father. I remember Pops said I could borrow one of his T-shirts since it would be oversized on me to cover up for my baptism. It did not click in my young mind that it was not as much a suggestion as it was a firm "you need to do this." I feel terrible for embarrassing myself and my family over something simple. I wish I could get rid of the memory. I wore a royal-blue tankini with a blue-and-green striped cover wrap around my waist.

I was underdeveloped and overweight, for which, as you recall from reading earlier on, I would be teased after the move.

As I stepped into the indoor inground pool in an assembly hall in Newburgh, NY, the water was clear blue and warm. There were two men—"brothers"—in the pool to conduct the baptisms. Poolside, there were women—"sisters"—in the locker room ready to assist with dry towels and give warm congratulations when you stepped out of the pool. And my family? Everybody was front and center. My nana (my mom's mom) came from Phoenix, AZ. My father drove his new family up from Maryland. It was a full family affair to watch my older brother and I get baptized on the same day.

His dip went well, smooth. When I was lifted out of the water, it was my worst nightmare. No one talked about it afterward, but I know it happened. My halter straps came loose. What little bit of breasts I had could have been completely exposed. Fortunately, I caught the straps, trying to hold it all together. I thought, *This is why a T-shirt was not merely a suggestion.*

And in hindsight, it is a good metaphor for how I eventually wound up when it came to sticking within the boundaries set for me. Somehow, I guess I was always meant to break free.

At nine years old, I did not understand the "brand" I was buying into fully. Those around me did not paint a specific enough picture. Why would they? My family's belief, especially my father, was that safety resided and existed only within the realms of the organization. As long as the family all stays (together), then we will all be okay. I know I let them down by not attending meetings or accepting their invitations to special events. I just could not get behind a brand that would not allow me to be my authentic self. I cannot stifle who I am. I will not backburner my passions or life goals.

If the world is going to end, I at least want to spend my time in it well. I am here for a good time, not a long time, as the phrase goes. I want my brand to be about something. I want to positively contribute and give back to my community. If there is a path to equity and inclusion in the workplace, I want to help forge it so future generations do not allow the corporate spaces to die because of old-fashioned thinking. If leaders do not have positive branding, how can we expect anyone to want to pick up the torch from us? If companies do not uphold their brand by executing fiercely on diversity, equity, and inclusion initiatives, how can we expect employees to be motivated daily? Our branding must be verifiable.

How do we go about branding? Think about what you know how to do well already, your skills. Write out a list. For kicks and giggles, redo your résumé. Have it ready; you never know when opportunity will come knocking on your door. Pro tip: Have a different résumé for every role to which you apply to highlight specific transferable skills relevant to the job post.

Can you write clear, effective, and influential communications? Are you able to coach a troubled employee through a tough time? Does your time management leave much to be desired? Do you easily overlook important items, or do you have an eye for the minuscule details? Have you ever controlled a room during an important presentation? Have you ever virtually controlled a room? Is your ability to solve problems above average? Can you design a logo or brand materials? Can your real-life talents come to work with you and be useful in the workplace?

Once you take time to have a real moment of self-reflection on your strengths, do the same with your weaknesses. Acknowledge your weaknesses and how they take away from your strengths if left unmanaged. Could you improve the efficiency and accuracy of your data entry? Are you as thorough as you think about setting expectations when you communicate with others? Are you good at starting projects but not finishing them? Know these things so you can describe how you can be an asset to your team(s), current and future.

How about the skills we do not think matter? Can your special talents be transferred to your regular job? For example, I did not recognize my stage performances as public speaking. I was discounting and discrediting myself. On paper, I've been "public speaking" for twenty-two years and counting. Crazy, right?

Seriously, think outside of the box. Do you create content for yourself on social media? Is it engaging? Do you have a large following? What kind of external network do you have that would benefit your professional career? Is there something you can do to connect your external network? How often do you engage in volunteer work? Maybe volunteering is your passion.

The idea of showcasing your passions and interests with your brand allows your talents to display who you are in a special way. Your private talents make you memorable. Whether you have a degree or not, when you work for any large, especially global, company, the talent pool is steeper than steep. It is imperative to stand out.

We may all have similar skills on our résumé: time management, networking, detail-oriented, complex problem solver, etc. It does not matter one bit. I was told one time to not even describe my organizational skills as "strong" or my time management as "excellent"—because if you get into the role and do not meet expectations of what the manager believes is "strong" or "excellent," the picture you painted is out the window. We each do things differently. Your level of "complex" or "organized" could differ from someone else's. It also depends on how your conversation flows during the interview and what the hiring manager's opinion and reception of you is.

Pay attention to the skills listed directly on the job posting. AI can shoot back great ideas for how you can pull the most important words out of a job posting or position to reshape your résumé. But be careful to only use what you can back or prove. Once you are branded a liar, it is pretty much a wrap.

Don't forget the skills attained from your life passions. This will set you apart from the competition because it lets people know what they are getting up front. Your leader will see you as a whole individual first and foremost. Then, if hired, your team will see you clearly. When applying for jobs in the past, I have even included a photo page of my family and interests and my writing portfolio to show my character. I am more than an employee, and you are as well.

We talked about communication contributing to transparency. It also applies to branding. How you communicate is part of your brand. If you tell it like it is, your brand can be considered "direct." You can be known for being receptive to feedback, someone who is super approachable. Feedback is anyone speaking up about something they believe could be different. If people cannot approach you for this, you are doing this leader thing all wrong. You can be known as a good listener or someone who interrupts others. (This last one is literally my biggest pet peeve.)

How can you respond to something before you hear the whole idea? Personally, I know I need to work on slowing down my thoughts. Fast-forwarding someone else's ideas by interrupting is just rude. A leader or not, this is unbecoming. A person who cannot allow you to finish your sentence or thoughts is immature. Yes, I can be rude and immature like the rest of them. I am not a perfect communicator. On the record, in front of the whole world, I will admit my partner is a better communicator at times than I am. *However*, the man is twelve years older than me—and he's an extrovert who's been a manager in his industry for years beyond my own experience. I am a highly introverted person who loves being at home and enjoys being alone (now), so there is still much to be explored on my end as it relates to communicating with people. I will never forget when one of my leaders told me something like "Good leaders do not make excuses and do not accept them." Eventually, I will have zero excuses. I *will* be a great communicator.

Is your brand one of a great communicator? Do you bring people together with the way you encourage others to participate in the conversation? Are you able to articulate yourself in a professional manner without having to change too much about who you are to express your perspective?

Being branded as a transparent, collaborative, and inspiring communicator is not too lofty an aspiration. It is very possible. Share what you know to be most important with your teams, what they need to know to be successful. Mind your timing and who is in the room. When it is your time to listen, really listen. Welcome diverse perspectives. Encourage creativity and participation. Show the vision with vigor and enthusiasm through storytelling, positive affirmations, and positive reinforcement.

You may believe me to be wild for saying this, but don't worry about code-switching as much. We all need to lean more into our professional voice. We shouldn't be bitter or upset about having to code-switch. Acknowledging it is one thing, and we have been doing this for years now. Why not let it go? If you look at it from a different perspective, it keeps us (BIPOC) safe, in a way, with how sensitive a climate we live in. This voice always needs to be on in a work setting. If you keep this voice on, it is second nature and a form of protection, in case someone takes something you say the wrong way. A personal favorite quote is "If you stay ready, you never have to get ready." Consistency is key. When you give different versions of your voice and personality, it can cause confusion.

Another area of concern is our online presence. Are you on all the socials? Who are you on these sites? Does your persona display someone capable of being professional, or is it less than becoming? If your employer looked at your page right now, what would they say? Do you align with their values and the company brand? Or could your activity get submitted to HR? Or worse yet, get you terminated?

If you cannot answer positively, I highly suggest you keep your pages private. There is a reason why this option exists. I have always kept my accounts private, until recently, but I have never fully agreed to the rule of leaders not connecting with those they lead. How will your people know who you are in real life if they never see your real life? Of course, you need to exercise caution here. I'd never want an employer or employee to question my character based on what I post or am tagged in on social media. The internet is forever.

What's out there should be a reflection of who you are, someone with good character.

When I am in the mood to post, if it is not uplifting, positive, fun, or motivational, I avoid social media. It keeps me from posting something I will regret. Have I reposted a subliminal message? Yes, indeed. This is as far as I go. No one will ever know who it is for or why. It will just seem as if I liked the quote and wanted to share.

In the last year, I have been doing 100-day fasts from Instagram, and this has helped so much. My focus improved. My productivity increased. It even revamped my feed, only showing recipe ideas, motivational speakers and quotes, what I call "funnies," fitness workouts, clothing designer pages, and news events (and oddly a lot of maternal/parenting hacks, as if I have children when I do not). Social media can be a blessing and a curse. The choice is yours. Make good decisions, and you will not have any worries.

Use social media for what it is, a tool. Social media is one of the best ways to market your brand. To intrigue people. To inform people. To inspire people. It is by far one of the most powerful resources available. Combine the use of social media with the genius of AI, and your brand could make you money in your sleep, depending on how you hustle. It allows someone to become interested in your brand based on something profound you may have said or done. It allows for a constant sharing of best practices when you really think about it. We all have come across a crazy hack we never knew existed, such as the time I realized the opener on the top of a canned soda, when turned for the openings to align, holds your straw. I learned this within the last three years. Shame on and laugh at me if you want.

Can your social media show you as an inspiring leader? One-hundred-percent. Have you posted what you do outside of work? The instrument you play? Your volunteer work? The crafts you create? The trips you take? Any house hacks? Any amazing food? What about as it relates to your day job? Are you a brand ambassador? Is there anything about your personal content that aligns with your company or employer? If there is anything you do outside of work that aligns you to your company's movement and vision, I encourage you to tap into it and make the most of social media in a responsible way.

If you need examples of responsibility, this might be a good time to explore your figurative "village" for mentors. No mentors? Time to put yourself out there for some good old-fashioned networking. Previously, networking meant you were going to a professional happy hour or conference. Now the popular "coffee chat" is the go-to. It has made it possible for remote workers like me to make friends and connections without being in the office.

This was useful for me when I was a call center trainer. I had a lot of time in a new environment. What better way to get acclimated than to get to know the leaders? After reviewing the hierarchy charts for the department and discussing my plan with my leader, I began my journey. I created a spreadsheet with three questions to host every conversation. I wanted to make sure my thirty minutes were spent well. Thirty minutes meant an average of ten minutes per question to discuss their background, current team, journey to leadership, and if they wanted to be in leadership at all. Every thirty minutes was well spent.

In six months, I met with a little under thirty leaders, including my director's peers and superiors. Their work experiences ranged greatly. Their family backgrounds were completely different. And most had degrees that had nothing to do with insurance. They gave me insight into their internal operations and showed me the importance of my team's role and my individual purpose. It was the first time I could connect the dots and understand what a well-oiled machine might look like when there is harmony. For every function, there was a training department with trainers who facilitated classes. We also had teams responsible for creating the curricula and modules. Before these conversations, I would have never known how small but mighty the operation was or who I could lean on for support during a project.

By familiarizing myself with the leaders, I fostered a good relationship with them. I was offered the opportunity to shadow and cross-train. This opened the door for me to be duly licensed as an adjuster and a producer (sales agent). I eventually had to surrender the producer license, but I gained visibility and understood where I fell in the grand scheme of things. I could see if this was the right role for me. How can you do what is best for the business when you do not know the business? Better question, how can you make your brand something people want to buy into if you do not know what the business needs? How can you know if you are in the right role if you do not know what everyone else does to keep the ship sailing smoothly?

Think strategically when networking and meet with as many leaders as you can. You do not have to stay within your own department or function unless there is a no open-door policy. I hope that by this point in society, we are done with closed-door environments.

Talking to leaders outside of claims makes for great connections. Sometimes it makes me sad to think I will never be able to progress outside of, or even upward in, claims. Then I remember I have people in my village who were in claims for twenty years before they transitioned to a different function. These examples tell me to keep pushing and to keep myself open. I'm already more than halfway there. It also shows support for my personal philosophy: If something is meant for you, it will happen. On the flip side, closed mouths do not get fed. With a balance of examples and guides to follow from my beloved village, I can keep giving my all, keep myself open, and keep putting myself out there too. Make no mistake. We still need to create our own opportunities. Some things just happen, while other things you *make* happen.

Your leaders seeing your hunger to consistently ask questions and take initiative shows them you mean business and can make for a strong brand. It shows your go-getter attitude. It shows you are confident in who you are. I brought an idea to a senior leader once, and it did not matter that the opportunity was a long shot because of the price tag; it gave them a glimpse into my brand and what I was willing to bring to the table.

I was initially going to speak this next section to Black women as a whole, but I would rather note this as a personal message to my unborn future children instead, especially my daughters. Please hear me with an open mind, and if not, feel free to skip to the next chapter. It may be for you; it may not be. Stereotypically, we are known for refusing to do things at work. "See, what I am not about to . . ." is a common phrase. I know because I use it when something doesn't make sense. In general, we are known for eye-rolling. We are known for sucking teeth. We are known for bad attitudes. We are known for visible facial expressions and body language to display discontent or dissatisfaction. We (Black people in general) are labeled as being late to everything, a term called "CP time" (Colored People Time), implying we show up when we want to, normally past the scheduled arrival time. Black people get branded angry if we show any kind of disagreement. Disagreement does not mean anger. It means we do not like the idea and likely have a better one.

But with Black women, our brands are affected by us the most. It starts outside of work. While we may be the most educated, buying yourself an education does not buy real talent, and it does not buy a personality people want to be around.

For anyone unwilling to acknowledge their faults, we cannot live this way anymore. We have to let shit go. We already have it bad enough because we worry about so many things our privileged counterparts and allies do not. Why are we making it worse for ourselves? As a Black woman, I have so much for which to be prideful. It is my aim to be better than the way I was yesterday, last week, a month ago, a year ago, ten years ago. When you aim high for yourself *and* your partner, the things around you will elevate, and eventually, so will your life.

Aiming high does not just look like going for the best salary or work conditions. It means work on your life more outside of work. No one at work will say it, so I will. The RBF (resting bitch face, as previously discussed) needs to be replaced with a smile as soon as possible. (I'm bad at this, and I know it.) Responding with emotions? Learn to check it before you open your mouth or send an email. Take it from a person who is quick to respond: It does not help anything. Still jumping to conclusions? Learn to listen to the whole story first. Stop assuming people are for your ruin because they did not like one thing you said or did and had the courage to tell you. You do not have to be best friends with people at work. But you will not have any friends or people who truly respect you if your brand reeks of a stereotypical Black woman. Find your happiness without being selfish. What can you do right now, today, that can bring you happiness without it affecting anyone else around you negatively?

Another thing I have noticed about us? If we are unhappy or want something, we will go to any length to get it, no matter if it hurts the people around us. For example, it is women who usually put divorce on the table first. Why? Because they are unhappy. We are all guilty of this kind of behavior. Where is the remorse? Why would we ever truly want to hurt people we love and who love us? Well, hurt people hurt people. Everybody has things going on, right? But everybody's "things" are not catastrophic or life-altering, needing immediate action. Be realistic. Blaming your hurt and unresolved issues on everything and everyone else is not okay.

Stop lying to yourself. If you can't back it up or remember the origin of who said or did what, it probably did not happen, which means you made it up. It is okay, my dear sister. Just laugh it off. I do this too, and all I can do is laugh at myself. When it all comes down to it, I theorize that we are all suffering from the remnants of DNA in us from our ancestors who were abused, raped, tortured, and murdered in front of one another. Children and husbands ripped from our great-great-great-grands. Because of this, I believe all Black people are inherently born with PTSD. This makes it difficult; however, we need to let go of what is deeply internal and strongly rooted in us. We think we cannot reach it. I say this is untrue. When we get past our past, we take ownership for who we are today and control over what is ours, our high-value brand.

We do not need to be mean to be heard. We do not need to be naked to be seen. We do not need to be loud to have an effective or clear message. We do not have to be fake to prove we are real. We do not have to run. We do not have to fear. We do not have time for the foolishness we create within ourselves to keep us from accomplishing what we have been for centuries at this point. If you have not noticed, Black women end up being mothers to all, nurturers to all, and, most of the time, saviors to all. Black women have been the working hands behind the scenes forever. We have made some amazing things happen for the world.

You cannot carry this weight if you have something blocking you, especially if the block is you. So, get out of the way and do the work to fix the negative undertones in your personality, not just your body. How you look on the outside means nothing to *anyone*. You want to be remembered for having a beautiful brain and beautiful outlook on life, not for just how you look or how much money you make. No one cares about this stuff at all. The internet is lying to you. Your authenticity is unlockable if you are willing to do the work on your inner person. The outside will follow. By doing the internal work, the person we bring to work every day will change, and you will see the difference in your interactions and overall outcomes.

Starting with something as simple as journaling helps. Talking to a therapist can also help. Spend time alone at home if you can, not to isolate but to do some deep introspection. We need to normalize spending time alone.

When speaking with peers, leaders, or direct reports at work, ask for their opinion and brutal honesty. Scary as this may be, you will learn a lot, and it will help you identify what areas you need to work on. Success and happiness are not race-specific. Do non-White people have a harder road to travel most of the time to get where they want to be? Yes. I wish people would stop being in denial about it. However, success and happiness are attainable for everyone who puts in the work. Think of you shooting your shot for what you want in life and inner happiness as a brand revamp.

By revamping your brand, starting from the internal person you know yourself to be and shifting to tackle the external, you will open doors previously closed to you. Your real life and work life will better align, which will allow the success and happiness you desire to be a reality.

So, who are you going to choose to be?

What is your brand's message? What do you want or need to say? Why is it important?

____

____

____

____

____

____

____

____

____

____

____

____

____

____

____

____

____

____

HOW TO SECURE YOUR AUTHENTICITY INSURANCE
WITH *Branding*

Build a strong, reputable, clear identity by standing on
business in person and online.

*Make the eyes focus and the minds wonder until you hear
the hands applaud.*

Chapter Five

Relationships

"Relationships are everything." This philosophy has brought my partner great success when connecting with people (before I was even a thought in his mind), whereas I had a bit of a late start in this regard. A wise man indeed. Being in the passenger seat to his driver seat, witnessing how he handles his relationships, has been interesting to watch. I am thankful to be with someone who cares so much about people, and I mean everybody, even those who do him wrong.

He has been in my passenger seat as I explore corporate. He was nervous for a while. I was always in the fast lane—and not afraid to change lanes. (Part of my climb, I was promoted vertically back-to-back within two years, which meant back-to-back swift changes without much time to settle.) In the end, when he saw how things were unfolding, he gave me credit for the hard work. He was initially adamant that I stay in one place, but he backed off gracefully, realizing the advice of my mentors was working well.

In times past, staying in one role was the right thing to do. If they could, most of our great-grandparents and grandparents would stay with the same company their entire lives and keep the same job no matter how bad. To be career mobile was not the thing to do. A career then meant you chose one role, one company, and this was your life. If you were a janitor, this is what you did until the day you died, but who knows how many great leadership opportunities people missed. Why not be a supervisor of the janitors, run a whole sanitation department or plant? Think *big*, you know? Maybe it was complacency or fear.

Today, a career can be seen as one touching all parts of a niche. You are valuable when you know all the pieces of a puzzle. Insurance is a humongous 1,000-piece puzzle. The larger a carrier you work for, the more you understand. There are positions you have never heard of or thought would belong within an insurance company. Each area you dive into has areas within that area and probably supporting areas for those areas. It is a *lot*.

How I have chosen to move has allowed me exposure and visibility from most aspects of a claim. I grew from a first-party-only adjuster to a first- and third-party total loss adjuster, from total loss adjuster to call center supervisor (I was promoted interim at first, then later applied to and earned the permanent position), from call center supervisor to call center trainer, and most recently from trainer to claims team manager, where I resumed work within an adjuster's setting. The claims team manager role allowed me to transition to commercial claims, a much hairier beast than personal claims. Maybe my partner was right to be nervous at first, but if you know insurance, you can see multiple sides to the niche of claims being touched here.

In the first two roles, I was a front-line employee. I investigated and resolved claims. In the third role, I oversaw a team of front-line individuals who created and assisted claims going to the adjusters for resolution. In the fourth role, I was responsible for training and assisting in the onboarding process for new hires who would be intaking calls to set up the claims for overall success. And in the fifth role, it is now my job to coach adjusters to properly investigate and resolve claims created by the call center. All the roles leading up to the fifth prepared me for this position. My consistency is there for everyone to see. This is something I am proud of that no one can take away from me. I may have gone backward to go forward, but I was always going up, and I did it without any letters or degrees behind my name. Seven grades in seven years.

Being a top performer was never in question when it came to my own authenticity insurance value. What I did not know for a long time was that there was more than being a top performer. You must meet new people and put in work with those people because *relationships are everything*. It takes a village to start a movement and make the ground shake.

What better way to make the ground shake in corporate than to be involved in employee resource groups (ERGs) if they are available to you. The whole purpose behind ERGs is to create safe spaces and allyships for people of varying demographics. It is a great space for volunteer roles to gain additional skills to aid in day-to-day roles or help build a new skill set to help earn a new role. I do not think people understand the extremely positive real-life effects ERGs can have. Say you have 5,000 people in your company, but only 1,000 participate in ERGs. What in the world are those other 4,000 people doing? Where are they?

ERGs allow people to feel and believe they are being heard. We talked about passions and talents earlier and how not everyone has found theirs yet. ERGs can be an outlet. Attending even one event could positively affect work and home life. You may learn how to better manage stress or feel inspired by a guest speaker's health and wellness talk.

ERGs have helped me in so many areas of my life. The biggest and most impactful result? I am able to create and maintain relationships. I have met mentors who have introduced me to people in their circles. In a couple years, I was organically ending up in important rooms with important people, which made me feel like wearing my extrovert hat was paying off. This also made me become a mentor because I wanted to support people how they needed it.

Before I knew it, in a few years, my village had about ten people I was regularly in contact with. I went to them for guidance when things were going wrong. I went to them for celebration when things were going right. I shared my aspirations with them. This was usually when they would graciously offer up their contacts and send introductory emails to help me make more connections. I shared my fears with them. Some, I had a cry with. Some, we shared a cry. My village carries so much weight to me, and I am so blessed and honored to have these people be my people. Mama, I got "people" now.

What does your village look like? Do you have one? Think of a village as your sanctuary. It includes people at work: your mentors, colleagues, or leaders. It includes people in your real life: your significant other, parents, friends, or siblings. Your village consists of everyone you seek advice from and those who know your general happenings. Should you think the population of your village needs improvement, here is my advice. There are connections we keep and maintain more regularly, and there are connections we maintain less regularly: the two-way streeters and the one-wayers.

For a while, this was a disagreement between my partner and me. He preached what it was like to have "lasting" friendships, stating that sometimes it is only one-way communication. Friendships have "seasons." When you reconnect, it is all love, all the time. It did not matter how much time passed; the relationship was solid based on two people showing up, friends who would defend you. His experience was valid, I told myself, but I am set up differently. And this difference of opinion is okay, one of many and certainly not the last or biggest.

Women are way different. We are all quite interesting creatures, not one of us being the same. Finding common ground is still rather difficult among many women trying to find friendship in other women. Everything is always a competition. And don't be in another age group completely—it's awful. The whole "women helping women" thing, especially in the Black community, can appear to be a facade. The facetiousness of women helping women is as easy to relate to as the example of how even women would rather watch the NBA than the WNBA historically. Women advocate that WNBA players should get paid the same as NBA players, yet we do not help the agenda. Hear me out: Is it not possible if more *women* filled the seats at WNBA games, this would add to the revenue of the organization and thus open the doors to the conversation of the players getting paid more money? Facts are, the NBA gets more screen time and higher paychecks because they get more supporters in general. Women could be the change here . . .

For the record, I have never watched a WNBA game and really do not pay attention to the NBA either. Basketball was not my favorite sport. I was an NFL girlie in a strictly Baltimore Ravens household. Overall, I am not too big on sports, mainly because . . . how are we paying athletes more than we are paying our teachers or doctors and nurses? When someone can answer this with sense, I will pay more attention to sports. No doubt, though, I will always show my hometown purple pride.

Now, if you are anything like me concerning friendships and supporting one another as women, you would respond, "Forget the one-way crap." A real friend is a person who is as interested in you and your life as you are in their life. A real friend commiserates with you. A real friend will tell you the truth when you do not like it because they want what's best for you, not someone who feeds you what you want to hear. A real friend does not let too much time go by before reaching out. With technology, there is no excuse—except lack of effort, care, interest, or all of the above.

People will be busy, always. Everyone is the main character in their own life movie. This makes it even more important for your village to be full of people who don't mind taking turns playing supporting roles. Like a quick text message to see how someone is doing when you know they are experiencing a tough time. There are not months where you do not hear from the other person. What kind of friendship is this? Is it one at all? Supporting roles looks like letting you choose what you do when you meet up half the time, helping your ideas come to fruition, genuinely wanting to see you win, giving you positive affirmations, and even being firm when necessary if a boundary is crossed, no matter how hard it may be. And vice versa. What your village is willing to do for you, you should be willing to do for them.

What really brings it all together to make the relationships in your village work is reciprocity. Receiving back what you put out absolutely matters. Reflect on your relationships. Stop playing or lying to yourself or making excuses for others. Are you okay with some of your relationships being one-way streets?

Everyone wants someone to show they care for them. Understand what the other person likes, values, and believes. Show your care with affirmations: sending a comforting message during a tough time or offering the biggest, tightest hug. Or simply listen more and talk less.

Be smart about who is in your village. You are who you surround yourself with, so choose wisely. Do the work to ensure your village is always under proper maintenance. To succeed, you need every person behind you to be fully present. The lead character is only as good as the supporting character(s). And when you get to where you are going, remember your supporters. Anyone who thinks they got where they are without their village is a fool.

I had to set myself up for success, yet my village was always there, backing me in their supporting roles. My first year as a claims team manager was unbelievable. I will never forget it. I realized, *I do not want to be in corporate when I'm forty.* The tests were always hard. There were no cheat codes. I did not have infinite lives. There were always traps waiting around corners. I absolutely believe it changed me for the better. I thought I knew where I was going before. I proved myself wrong in surviving my first year in commercial claims. Yes, I am okay. I made it and still have so much to learn.

On this journey, my village keeps me on my toes. They keep me inspired. They give me useful tools. I always leave a meeting feeling better than when I went into it. To keep this consistent, I balance my team's biweekly one-on-one conversations. On the weeks I do not meet with my team, I meet with my village. I have been meeting with the same folks for a few years, which has allowed me the pleasure of meaningful and impactful conversations. We may not always keep the same cadence; however, I know they are always an email, instant message, or text message away.

Mentors are there for *you*. What are your personal and professional goals? Where do you see yourself in five years? Where do you see yourself in ten years? What are your biggest areas of concern? How can you improve your weaknesses? How can you unlock self-awareness? Are you looking for a temporary work situation or permanence and stability? Is your progress noticeable? Is your plan realistic, or do you need help mapping things out?

A good mentor makes you *think*. A good mentor *pushes* you. A good mentor *challenges* your reality. If you want to be better, a good mentor understands the assignment and shows up with their whistle ready to blow it loud in your face. A good mentor recognizes there is always a moment for humility and always an opportunity to go outside the lines to make something *bigger, brighter, better*. Before you know it, you will have a masterpiece. The masterpiece will be you and whatever you get your hands on.

You will be a masterpiece transcending time and space because you will never be "done." You will never be "finished." You will never reach your end. Having a mentor makes the opportunity to become a masterpiece more possible. You will thrive and evolve. Should having a mentor count as a form of social self-care? Yes, yes, yes. Whenever I can mentor, I love doing it because I enjoy filling someone else's cup. It fills me simultaneously.

Do not forget one thing. Mentorships and sponsorships are not the same thing. In the simplest explanation, a mentor is someone who will coach you to your goal, like preparing you for an interview. A sponsor is someone in your village who is willing to vouch for you to a hiring manager, like writing a recommendation letter or providing an endorsement. Both mentorships and sponsorships are extremely important. Understand their differences.

What some of us may not want to realize is that our relationships outside of work could be standing in our way. Whether you're in a romantic relationship or you are a parent, the most important relationship in the whole entire world has to be the one you have with yourself.

You cannot work for anyone if you are not working for you. You cannot help anyone until you help yourself. You cannot pick someone else up when you are in a hole. You cannot heal someone else until you heal yourself (or at least start the journey). You will be incapable of loving others until you have figured out how you need to be loved. You will only bring chaos if you do not find internal peace. This responsibility belongs to no one except you.

I know I cannot function on a day where my anxiety is high. It weakens my attention span. On these days, I will call out before I let anyone see me slip or make a mistake. If I am unable to control my emotions, I could be leading my team down the wrong path. For this and other reasons, I work hard to keep my mental health in check. If I am not working for me, how am I able to sign in and work for someone else?

I will admit my romantic relationship started in an unorthodox way. After almost ten years, it makes me proud to see how far we have come. Hindsight will always be twenty-twenty. You cannot help but reflect. Introspection is how we grow. When we first started "talking," I was in one of my most vulnerable states. I was fresh out of my father's house and working a tough job I was not ready for. With my family trauma, you would think I would have been in therapy immediately and consistently. At the time, though, the company only covered a few free sessions with a counselor. I went through those visits quickly and could not afford additional bills, so my mental health was on the back burner. Simultaneously, my now partner was also in a very vulnerable place.

Unfortunately, my younger self did not understand the importance of mental health. I was not ready to be the shelter he needed because I had not created my own. And he was not ready to be mine because his world was falling down around him. To my own demise, I dove headfirst into his and his family's life and crashed around like a bull in a china shop, with zero instincts or wherewithal. Year after year, I made misstep after misstep. It took time for me to slow down long enough to recognize the work I had to do on my mental health. Today, I would not say I am all the way healed. It is easier now, though, to live with my wounds freely for all to see.

Until you have helped yourself, there is no one you can truly support. And love?

Love is such a dream and a nightmare.
Love is confusing and enlightening.
Love is blurry yet clear.
Love is sacred and pure.
Love is treacherous and manipulative.
Love is relative and subjective.
Love is joyous while painful.
Love is depressing and lonely.
Love is angry yet capable of being kind.
Love is a commodity, yet some will sell theirs for a dollar, label, or status.
Love is not blind to effort.
Love is enduring the most intense and severe tribulations.
Love is happiness and contentment.
Love forges the way because love is forgiveness, and everyone needs forgiveness.
If you do not know how to love yourself, you cannot love anyone else.

We [Black people] have beautiful, wonderful examples of long-lasting relationships, but the powers that be do not want you to believe Black families stay together. Search the most recent divorce rate for yourself. Statistics lead with the negative and leave out the positive to try to exacerbate their claim. Black love is a real thing for a lot of people, including me. You have some who literally refuse to date outside the race, let alone marry. A couple sharing their entire lives is special and a shining example of unconditional love. To grow together. Create life together. Have fun together. Experience tough times together. Cry together. Die together.

Trust me when I say I understand trauma. I understand feeling unloved. I understand living in a house where you are not wanted. I understand being ignored and neglected. I understand involuntarily being alone. I understand having panic and anxiety attacks. I understand the stomach pains and migraines from the lack of self-care because no one taught it to you. I understand not wanting to be alive anymore. I understand being hurt and stripped of dignity.

By taking the time to heal and process your trauma, you minimize your negative output. Your healing looks like you strengthening your ability to control you. Control your emotions. Control your habits. Control your surroundings. Control your programming. Control your relationships. Control your career. Control your life. We naturally feel better when we are in control. Doing things your way makes you feel comfortable. Remember, though, when you want to grow and gain more control over your life, you *will* be uncomfortable.

If you are already comfortable, you may not have a desire for more. You have lifelong climbers; then, you have climbers who set their destination and stay there when they arrive and settle. Their destination is their safe space, where they feel comfortable, so they may not wonder or care if there is anything else. Is there anything else when you "make it"? Those who answer "yes" probably seem insatiable. I see them as misunderstood and simply seeking discomfort for the sake of personal and professional growth, for the sake of breaking mental chains and really healing, for the sake of tearing down barriers to unblock and unlock blessings, for the sake of ending poor family cycles and recreating the pathology of one's family line.

Do you think any real movement is started in a state of comfort? No! People who think there are no problems do not look for problems to solve, especially not for others. People who are at the very top rarely seem to look down from cloud nine. If it does not affect them, why does it matter? This mindset angers me. I am a firm believer that when you make it to the top, you should pull others up with you. Let there be a way or make a way. If you are the only one in your village who is successful, you might as well still be at the bottom. Until those around you are as elevated, your success, I'm sorry to say, doesn't count as much as you think it does. Truly unthreatened, powerful, and successful people help others to get to their level; they don't stay at the top and keep it all to themselves. And they certainly don't look down on others, watching the struggle of those who are doing their best to pull themselves up, popcorn in hand, as if it is entertainment.

I guess it depends on a person's ride to the top. If you did not have to scrape by or put in much effort, your view may be from a very privileged lens. Much like if you have never experienced poverty, you will be very disconnected from many who started poor and had to lift themselves up to reach where they are currently. A good mentor of mine, a graduate of Rutgers Women's College, reminded me that lighting someone else's candle does not extinguish your own light, which taught me that it can't hurt to help others shine alongside you. If anything, it shows your luminousness.

As leaders, it is our responsibility to connect people, not create the divide. It is our job to inspire, guide, teach, develop, aid, and support our people. Reaching where you want to go does not make you a success if you don't pull people up with you. If you are only ever worried about you, how good is it for your village? What good is this mindset doing for the world?

Hopefully, your village will keep you grounded and in tune with yourself because they remind you of what you say and hold you accountable. Holding someone accountable does not mean you are policing or parenting. When someone shares a goal with you, as a good friend, you bring it up and discuss their progress. You may offer your assistance. If they take you up on it and the task is within your power, you step up and help, zero questions. Well, maybe not zero. There will always be questions. You get the point.

You are nothing and will go nowhere without healthy relationships. They are part of what underwrites your authenticity insurance. You need relationships to be strong, harmonious, and in alignment with who you are now and who you see yourself becoming in the future. Not all of them will make you comfortable. Not all of them are there for your comfort. Some are there by way of necessity, and the necessity could be to make you uncomfortable so you actually experience a mistake or failure. It is only from mistakes and failures that we are capable of understanding what it means to grow. If you are always perfect and appear to have always done everything the "right way," you are the most inexperienced of us all. If you don't know how to get it wrong, you will never truly appreciate getting it right.

Experience comes from failing. As you fall, you have no choice other than to reflect on your ascendance. The phrase "My life flashed before my eyes" is appropriate here. As you are falling, be it from a bike, a horse, stairs, a building, or plain grace, you may find yourself watching as your brain plays a quick visual clip of everything you have done. Let you survive, a common feeling is one of change. You desire a difference in how you live your day-to-day life. A very powerful epiphany occurs when you learn from experiencing failure.

It may take a while to get back to where you were; however, on the way, you get to pick up all the things you missed on the first try. You strengthen yourself. You expand your knowledge base. You earn more trusting companions. You might even learn that the previous path was not the path you were supposed to be on anyway. Sometimes, the universe hits reset for you because it sees something bigger and better out there.

Those still around after a crash are the real companions. Anyone around after multiple crashes, well, that's family. Don't feel guilty when relationships do not work out. I had to learn that I am not for everyone, and everyone is not for me.

So, how fortified is your village?

What would you want to learn from someone outside your
own generation?
If you are older, what would you want to learn from
someone younger?
If you are younger, what would you want to learn from
someone older?
Find the intersectionality.

____

____

____

____

____

____

____

____

____

____

____

____

____

____

____

HOW TO SECURE YOUR AUTHENTICITY INSURANCE
WITH *Relationships*

Fill your village with people rooting for you as much as
you are rooting for them to win.

You are not for everyone. Everyone is not for you.

Chapter Six

Imagination

Are you a big-picture thinker? Insurance and other aspects of corporate America are not all boring, not when you have an imagination to help you see the bigger picture. When you are capable of being innovative, you unlock many solutions to a problem. You can see from all sides. I have had the opportunity to come up with helpful resources to put teams on track to solve their problems by thinking outside the box and going outside of normal parameters, sometimes with permission, other times having to ask for forgiveness. As a bonus, I have watched my partner on his entrepreneurial endeavors. Choosing between working for someone else or working for yourself to follow your life's work and purpose is a tough decision. It is not for the weak or faint of heart. And it certainly takes a lot of willpower and imagination.

Let us be honest with ourselves. What happened or what is happening to our imagination as we get older? It probably got sucked up into anxiety's vacuum, right along with our joy, once we crossed the adult threshold. Everything about using our imagination now after a certain age feels childish and wrong, especially at work, but why? Why does it feel improper to utilize what is basically a free talent? Your brain has its own built-in resource center for problem-solving, only requiring you to use it to keep it fresh. Our imagination is what keeps the world running because people are bravely coming up with new ideas every day to sustain our survival, economy, education systems, governments, everything. Granted, not all ideas are good ideas. However, if we stop using our imagination, we lose our curiosity. If we stop being curious, we lose our imagination. They work hand in hand. If we lose our curiosity and our imagination, we experience the same problems in a loop. History will repeat itself. It will be a never-ending cycle. If we land in a never-ending cycle, nowhere is where we are going. Whether you are old or young, whether you have been working since last year or working since last century, your imagination and ability to be curious carries so much weight. Your ability to maintain a growth mindset is dependent upon your use of imagination and curiosity.

Why do curiosity and imagination work together? Curiosity gets the imagination started, usually with a question. As children, we had questions about everything. Our favorite follow-up question was "why," never satisfied with the initial answer. As adults, we should ask "why" as much as possible. Do not be afraid to allow your imagination to partner with your curiosity. We must make educated decisions about how we live and work. When properly balanced and utilized together, curiosity and imagination are at the center of accessing the creative spirit we all have and unlocking your true power. Knowledge is power. The more you stay curious and open, the more you learn. The more you learn, the more powerful you become.

It's important to ask questions in your day-to-day work and when involved in ERGs. While there are great benefits to ERGs, be aware of programming and content. Keep in mind how these volunteer groups were probably implemented or approved. It *may* have become more diverse over time. The politics of ERG leadership is stressful. You could strive for a leadership role and be denied because your role does not reflect what the interviewer deems as transferable skills. This makes it hard because it contributes to the endless cycle of people hearing "you need experience to be a leader." Hearing this in your day-to-day job *and* in a volunteer space can be discouraging. It's disheartening to deal with rejection from all sides. Never fear, though, because there is always a way in. You need to use your imagination to find the path.

For the sake of this conversation, we will give props to our legacy leaders, those who have been with a company twenty-plus years, and dub everyone else with less tenure as the next generation. An occasional downside to legacy leaders is the complacency and pushback for new things. You can find yourself in a room with people who seemingly share the same brain and perspective. There may be a lack of diversity in background, culture, and experiences. The positive side is that there are so many cheat codes you can learn. Often, the things you experience were already dealt with, and all you have to do is find the person willing to share how they made it through so you may learn from them. There are so many lessons found when you ask the right people the right questions.

On the flip side, the next generation (myself included) holds the opportunity to have patience, compassion, and tactfulness for open dialogue with more experienced leaders about their shortcomings, if we ever want a shot at being one of tomorrow's leaders. It may be off-putting to always feel looked down upon or left out of communication, sure. No one likes being the last to know anything. The truth is, it is not the legacy leaders who will need to break systemic issues. It is the responsibility of the next generation to put in the work.

These are big shoes to fill, and the crown is extremely heavy. Whether you carry a title of leadership or not, your work environment is 50 percent your responsibility. Do not think in the same fashion as some legacy leaders, to show up only for a check. While I believe legacy leaders deserve to take it easy if they choose to, they may be creating spaces of resentment. When you are not open to new ideas or increasing diversity, you are making the conditions less enjoyable. It will be hard to earn trust from the next generation. Legacy leaders, you must care all the way to your last day. You cannot check out before passing along what you know. On your part, this is irresponsible. Why put a damper on your own visible legacy?

Next generation, *ask more questions*! I yell this at myself daily. There are work-arounds for many things already in place; however, these legacy leaders are not necessarily going to share if you do not ask. We cannot assume we know everything. Legacy leaders have more experience. Use this to your advantage. Soak up as much as possible. Shadow as much as possible. Inquire about everything. Make no assumptions or conclusions. Keep your mind open.

Whether you want to be a leader or not, having help will always be easier than going the entire way on your own. Some may like or not mind the challenge of the journey, while others prefer to work smarter, not harder. Even I have played a video game straight through and then gone back to play side quests for extra points or money, to go back to the last level to win it even better.

I am also living proof of this. My partner is twelve years older than me. My survival through my twenties was hard. I had to work through a lot of communication and listening skills, and I admit things would have been more difficult without him. Being able to bounce off someone who has already had certain experiences has been a great benefit.

When you find someone, whether in a personal or professional setting, willing to help you, learn what you can from them, go talk to your village about it, and go from there. Do not sit on the information; put it to work. Evaluate it, examine it, meditate on it. Really think it through. How can you apply the advice, suggestion, or story to your situation?

Consulting with my village, I know they see the same flaws I see. They saw and experienced it first. They know the cycle because they have been upward, backward, sideways, and diagonal through it. The injustice of departmental politics exists no matter where you work. A lot of companies, before this whole war on diversity, equity, and inclusion, set metrics and measurements to benchmark success, such as a certain percentage of women or a specific demographic (not just race) being given more opportunities. The push for diversity, equity, and inclusion is slowing down. There are even people replacing the "diversity, equity, and inclusion" in DEI with "Didn't Earn It." Can you believe the disrespect?

Next generation, do not be disheartened by this. We are in control of ourselves. There is always work to do within you in the interim. You will never be perfect. This makes your work cut out for you. Use your imagination and curiosity to assess your self-awareness, strengths and weaknesses, reactivity to pressure, long-term career and life visions, ability to collaborate, and whether you can prioritize the balance between your work and personal life.

Whatever the legacy leaders leave behind, you will feel the effects from a leadership or individual contributor standpoint. It is not dissimilar to the real world. Everything the boomers set in place worked well for them, but not so much for everyone who came after them. Can you believe some people will *never* own a home? The American dream was real once. Now it is harder than ever to crack the code. I say fight for your dream, whatever the dream may be. Do not let your imagination and curiosity die. If the next generation does not take the reins responsibly, we will be in for a terrible downfall.

You need the knowledge of legacy leaders and innate curiosity to do big things like tend to a workforce's mental health. There was a survey released at work in early spring one year. It asked if you would recommend working here. It asked about negative and positive moment(s), whether you felt burned out, your stress levels, and if you thought your work had meaning. It was not too surprising to learn that so many were experiencing high stress. Holding a solution-based mindset in the moment, my imagination went on a tangent. I looked at all the content produced by the various ERGs. I evaluated various groups' programming consistency and topics, and I came up with some ideas I believed would work. I pitched these ideas in an interview to be a committee leader for a group to which, visibly, my skin tone showed me to be an ally, yet internally and according to 23andMe, I was actually a descendant. Saying this fact in the interview and my wanting to connect with this side of myself by volunteering fell on deaf ears.

I was rejected and given a counteroffer to be part of the committee. Instead of being hurt and in my feelings, I allowed my imagination to take me to a place where productivity manifests. I chose to view "no" as a "not yet" or "not right now." I tell myself this because hearing "no" can make you feel really low. Hearing "no" at work took its toll on me, thankfully not before I allowed an external talent to show up at work.

In 2021, I wrote, produced, and hosted a podcast on Spotify called "A Thousand Words or Less." I only did about thirty episodes, and it lasted about nine months. The purpose was to give a positive message to my local community. I provided current events along with a Black History moment. I challenged listeners to try new things and to look inward for power. One of the segments on these ten- to fifteen-minute episodes was called "To Be Enlightened Is to Be Informed." In a short time frame, I interviewed community members, working professionals, who were able to speak intelligently about their crafts and industries. I encouraged people to open their minds to being the source of energy and stimulation they need to accomplish anything to which they set their mind. Never did I think I would be applying this kind of skill in a workplace. I did though.

I spoke very openly and vulnerably about my mental health conditions on a panel one year. A senior leader attended and sent a follow-up email saying that I should try my hand at a committee I never even knew existed in one of the ERGs focusing on mental health. The ERG itself was always on my radar; however, the specificity on mental health pulled me in. First, I was honored this leader showed up because they made me feel supported and seen. Second, following up with the names I was provided paid off. I attended a committee meeting. The rest was history. During the first meeting, I found an amazing partner with whom I would have many collaborations.

This partner was geared up to do a podcast too. Kismet. You may be shocked to know my partner technically falls into the legacy leader group. You may also be shocked to know the way we work is literally a perfect balance, especially for Black women. Yes, I said it. No need to act like we all get along. It's better to be honest and admit we don't.

I am so thankful this was not the case here and we could go into planning heavily and intentionally. We asked the tough questions about our intended audience and ourselves. What were each other's top skills, and where could we each use a little support? I saw a much more reserved approach from her, whereas I showed a bolder in-your-face approach. She would admit it was a quality she liked in us young folk, not being afraid to say what others might hold back. Me? I loved the grounding I received from her, not dissimilar to the grounding I received in my relationship with my partner. With our mutual understanding, shared common goal, and rolling imagination, we created content with the goal of releasing episodes regularly. We planned crossover events and interviews with other ERGs.

Our first set of releases was a short series released during Black History Month on self-care. There are six areas of self-care. We created six ten-minute episodes. Each episode included examples of a type of self-care, a color representing the emotion behind it, a guided meditation with two minutes of affirmations, and available company resources designed to help. As a result, we received great support and feedback. Our imagination did not stop at self-care. With the entire year's outline on paper, it was all a matter of execution.

In a matter of months, we had an interview with one of the company's in-house therapists who candidly expressed how stress negatively affects *everything*. It was a conversation where we shared personal details to reveal our intentions behind the show to the audience. We had our reasons for why therapy needed to be part of our lives, and we wanted our listeners to do the same kind of reflection. We encouraged folks to get help and be there for people who needed it.

We also had the pleasure of interviewing a community member of the same ERG who was pivotal in gaining accessibility features to one of our main office locations. This employee shared their battle with a physical condition and how they did not let anything hold them back from speaking up about the need for accommodations for wave buttons, appropriate seating, and more. It was a truly inspiring conversation.

These interviews prepared us for the biggest opportunity of all. I thought, *What if we could score a C-suite executive to come on the show? Then we could really have a conversation about the mental and physical health of our employees.* I asked my partner if she was okay with my shooting my shot and inviting them to the show. She agreed, and once she tweaked my draft email invitation, I hit send. When you *stay* ready, you do not have to *get* ready. Never show up empty-handed when you want someone to buy into your idea or buy into you. It took some time, and the wait was nerve-racking. It was worth it. We got our yes, and the planning was underway.

None of it would have happened without asking questions. I allowed my imagination to push past assumptions that a C-suite executive would never make time. We *created* a table for both of us and invited powerful players to figuratively break bread and share in an important conversation we believed would mean a lot to a lot of people. And it did. As a personal accomplishment, it was the first time one of our shows was shared with the entire global organization on the company's main intranet site.

With that story, again, I urge you not to allow anxiety to strip you of your imagination and curiosity. Most of the negative thoughts we think could happen will never really happen. Why? Because when you only aspire to do good things, good normally follows. I am not saying bad things will never occur. I lean hard into the real effects of karma.

Do not let hurtful, untrue narratives blind you from seeing the bigger picture: *you.* Remember the force you are. Remember the things you can do that no one else can. Remember the village you have behind you. Remember the important and difficult self-work you are doing. Remember the superpower(s) you have been sitting on, sharpening as you patiently wait your turn. Remember to *use your imagination.*

How will you stand out? Show yourself capable of creative problem-solving to lead to real innovations. Innovations are not only new products. Innovations are new *ideas, processes, methods.* You may not have the next best idea for a new "thing." Yet, you could be sitting on the very idea or process necessary to boost productivity and, by default, profitability.

Curiosity makes you ask the questions necessary to identify the roots of your problem. Curiosity outfits you with the ability to cast a net far and wide to gather information to brainstorm new processes. Your free, wonderful imagination will allow you to go for the unknown because it might work out. Recreating the wheel can be time-consuming. Working smarter, not harder, can still bring innovation. Don't listen to the doubters and haters. They will always exist.

As human beings, regardless of gender, sexual orientation, religion, disability, or race, it is everyone's responsibility to do the right thing. Hiring voices with different backgrounds can only boost innovation and creativity. Leadership should not hire the same, tired person repeatedly. Legacy leaders who hire their look-alikes may say, "The talent is not anywhere else" or "This was really the best candidate," and they are so full of shit. If your team is all of one thing, your team will never be as good as a diverse team. When I was a trainer, we had every race background, with each race represented by one person from each gender. Easily the best team I have ever been on, period.

Leaders, please stop acting as if a degree means more than actual experience. The minute you tell a recruiter you only want candidates with a degree, you cut your talent pool. Stop overlooking well-tenured people who have given years of their life to a company. You are missing out on real talent. Someone who has run a small business has business acumen. This is what I love about entrepreneurship. It is real hands-on experience. Someone who has only ever been in school does not have more promise than someone who has been running their own business for years. We should be looking at individuals without a degree with longing to want to develop them. Give them the opportunity to do something bigger because a motivated person gets the best work done.

What I am saying is for recruiters too. Look beyond the degree already. For. Every. Role. You never know who will apply. Take the time to review *everyone*. Stop leaving it to the computer to screen talent. Pick up the phone to have a conversation. I miss the days when all recruiters were nice and genuine about people finding the right roles. Nowadays, it seems like you do not even receive a response when you ask for feedback on why you did not move forward in the process.

Diversity is noticeable when you bring an entire unit together. Leaders, please communicate all opportunities to everyone in your workforce. Why allow resentment to foster in your own camp? People can see when the same people receive the same special treatment.

Something I helped implement in my unit was *development days*. Once per month, each adjuster was able to have one day off from receiving claims, and they would not have to be logged into the phones. Development days could be used to catch up on overdue work or emails, study for insurance designation courses, attend ERG events, etc. We did a three-month pilot followed by a survey. Everyone spoke about their improvement in desk management, the quality of their work, and their participation with ERGs.

Thanks to an extremely positive reaction (82 percent satisfaction rate based on about 75 percent of the unit participating in the survey), the pilot went permanent. We created an equitable learning space. By continuing, we will be walking the walk in our push for a culture where employees believe they have the proper support and are respected and valued. Employees who feel valued and respected believe they belong. When employees believe they belong and no one in particular is receiving special treatment, they will be more inclined to do the right thing and get their work done. Increased productivity equals increased profitability. This math will always math.

The people in the room *with* leaders? I'm also talking to you. Accountability is everything. We must hold ourselves accountable to doing the right thing. Doing the right thing might look like holding your leader accountable. If you do not understand how your success is measured, hold your leader accountable to showing you. Ask for examples. Do not be afraid to ask your leader "why." If you do not like the answer, do not be afraid to challenge them—respectfully.

We must use our imagination to ask more questions. We need to hold ourselves accountable for the atmosphere of our workplaces. We need to hold ourselves accountable for the atmosphere of our volunteer spaces within our workplaces. For the ERGs, we need senior leaders to be more involved, with the goal of coaching and developing those who are looking to gain more experience outside their day-to-day roles.

Senior leaders' support for ERGs shows front-line workers that they will not be penalized for their participation. As I was being interviewed for a leadership role recently in a volunteer space, we talked about my vision for me in the role and how I would accomplish creating something from nothing. Most volunteer interviews went like this for me. There was always a need for structure, something I love to create. Part of what I shared was creating a campaign specifically for senior and executive leaders to "sign" their support for employees wanting to explore ERGs. This document would motivate people to try them out and ensure there would not be retaliation if they missed *one* hour per month to join an event. This could improve people's career experiences, like ERGs did mine, and allow for evolution instead of a revolution within the workforce.

Another thought I had but haven't necessarily shared until now is this: Instead of the optional approach concerning newsletters, why not have every ERG send their newsletters to all employees within the region or area? Each group brings something different to the table. News is news. Everyone should be equally informed.

Easily measure growth by assessing the attendance and

membership count a year from now. When a company's reports claim they meet their diversity rate, yet they are not meeting the goal, ERGs can be a source of recourse. These are some of the most freeing spaces for people to use and flex their imagination for the improved workplace experiences.

Was there an increase in productivity? Were more projects completed than the prior year? Were KPIs met or exceeded versus the prior year? How is work attendance? How is turnover? Was there an increase in savings and profitability? Has the atmosphere changed? How is employee satisfaction?

So, do you see the bigger picture now?

What problem do you believe you could solve right now?
Why? How would you do it?

HOW TO SECURE YOUR AUTHENTICITY INSURANCE
WITH *Imagination*

Stay curious, never closed.

Be a daily learner.

Chapter Seven

Empathy

Empathy is the ability to understand and share someone else's feelings. You see their point of view and understand how they may feel. If you have no personal experience in relation to the matter, your imagination will allow you to think about the situation as if you were them. It is way different from sympathy. No one wants to be pitied.

I struggled with empathy for a long time. My upbringing was the source of this pain. For almost a decade, I believed no one could empathize with my home experiences. I did not have a safe space. Any time I tried to safely vent and let out some of my emotions, the message would get back to my father's house. Surprisingly, this happened a few times as an adult, too, where what I said while venting in distress would get back to my house and cause more problems, even when I asked for it to be kept between me and the other person. When I was a child, I wondered if who I would vent to would have stopped going to my father or his wife if they knew it resulted in worse conditions for me. Many times, from child to adult, I have needed someone to shut up and listen, not solve. Everybody needs a friend.

When I entered the work world, I was completely jaded. As a 911 call-taker, at only eighteen, lack of life experience made me as scared as the person on the other end of the call.

Transitioning into the insurance business, the phone calls were smoother, though some were still difficult. In claims, the job is still to talk to people in distress all day. It is a different animal, still an animal, nonetheless. I struggled to connect to customers. I had no patience for entitlement. Not all customers were assholes; some were sweethearts. For me, it was the lack of accountability for peoples' accidents that made it difficult. How does it make sense for you to be the one making demands if you caused this loss? And, how can you yell at the person you called to help you? Can anyone make this make sense?

It took me years to really access empathy. I am still not always good at being empathetic. My partner will confirm. I can admit when you are dealing with what feels like a lot of pain to you, you get engulfed in it. You suffocate. When there are not a lot of people who can relate, it is isolating. A big problem to you can be a small problem to someone else. What helped me change was knowing that empathy is at the core of every connection. There is not a relationship or friendship or human interaction that does not require empathy.

Businesses are made up of human beings. Every human being has their own life outside of work, their own problems, struggles, agenda, feelings about world events, ideals about how life should be, perspectives, and overall life outlook. If you dehumanize a company and leave emotion out of it, you will never truly be a successful leader.

Be aware of others' experiences. My experience as a Black woman, knowing what it feels like to be underprivileged and underserved, may significantly differ from a White woman or a man, even if our upbringings were similar. This is why I believe the sooner you better understand empathy, the sooner you will understand we are surrounded by disparities, gaps, and inequities. Racism and prejudices still exist, as we have seen many who were hiding and filtering their true nature who have come right back out into the open to show their true colors as of late.

Please, I am begging you, take your blinders off. Stop saying you do not see color. This has always been the wrong thing to say. Color and race have effects on literally everything. When you can, allow people of other races, genders, and sexualities to share. And really listen. If you get in the mood to fact-check, feel free. Listen first, though. You will learn something. Diversity, equity, and inclusion were not only for Black people, like everyone assumed. As a result, right now, there are many people regretting their poll choices, realizing DEI was for anyone who was not a White male.

DEI created the space for empathy. And empathy is applicable everywhere. Empathy allows you to see other people's perspectives. When you have employees who believe their opinion is worth something and they can freely express their feelings, you are adding to overall morale. It takes time to build trusting relationships. It takes time to build engagement. It is our responsibility to try.

Circling back to the feelings wheel, start someplace simple. "Pick a word to describe your mental state right now." Do not forget the follow-up question of "why." Allow them the opportunity to finish their statement. Paraphrase their answers to affirm you heard what they said and ask another question. They have the floor. It is their moment to be open and share—and your moment to be open to shutting up and listening. Overall, when people feel they can talk to you, they want to talk to you more. Your conversations may even get longer. You are modeling active listening skills. You are leading the way for them to share new perspectives. The individual work you do will be visible in large group settings too.

How do we enhance the customer experience? How can we create trustworthy employee experiences? What does it take to attract and retain the best talent? How do we maintain safe spaces in unique ways? How can we maintain balance within our teams?

When your teams can focus without you, it leaves you to the bigger picture. I will always love a good planning session. Maybe it's the Virgo in me. I will never say leaders have one-hundred-percent control of their environments. With people involved, you can only manage their personalities and set proper expectations. What can you control? You can reduce overall issues and internal discrepancies in an environment where empathy is evident. You can prevent misunderstandings. You can hear an employees' concerns without becoming defensive. You allow for people to help you get to the root of issues.

Issues can be right in the open and hidden at the same time. How quickly those things come out will depend on your approach. When people trust you, they give it all to you. They will give you their anxieties, fears, desires, ideas, problems, wins, and frustrations. You may even laugh at how easily some folks will dry snitch on others because they know you will help exact change.

Maybe it's a teammate not pulling their weight. An adjuster being behind could mean the rest of the team receives their overflow calls. Every worker carries the same frustration toward an individual who does not take care of their customers. Resentment grows in this environment.

What I discovered, in my situation, by practicing an active listening ear was that the previous leader did not address the lack of productivity with the proper steps of corrective action. They created more work for themselves, covering up the performance issues instead of holding the adjuster accountable. I did not want anyone to feel like they were cleaning up after another person. No one likes feeling this way. As a result, in a matter of months, we had an entirely new team. Performance improved, and people who previously wanted to leave decided to stay and learn, moving up the ranks or trying a new departmental role. Empathy, when used wisely, can transform a team.

Keep in mind, the bottom line is Benjamins—for Corporate America, which has little space for weakness, let alone empathy. I learned this the hard way during COVID-19.

I was living with my partner's family. We moved in about six months after his dad passed away. By the time COVID-19 happened, we had been there for a year. Everything happened quickly.

In January 2020, a few months prior to the shutdown, we were informed our offices would be permanently closing in six months due to changes in our company's real estate. The office was a few floors in an office plaza, not the whole building. This physical change came with personnel changes. Managers and adjusters were informed of their impending layoff, and whoever was left would be transitioning to a permanent work-from-home status.

With metric performance changes after the first quarter, I was experiencing so much change at work and home. I remember breakdown after breakdown. I remember telling my partner's family I was having negative thoughts. I remember the visit to our county crisis center. I remember the voicemail I left my manager one day when I could not return to work.

This was four or five years into my career with the company. The year prior, I earned top performer twice back-to-back, locally and nationally. I enjoyed the pleasure of traveling across the country to collaborate and problem-solve with one of our support teams. I hadn't had a bad year yet. I was only getting stronger. I was so grateful to not be part of the cuts when our office shut down.

A humbling moment when my new manager approached me with their manager. I was too young to notice the energy in the "room" (we were virtual). It was clear I was about to get my first write-up. I had never had a senior leader pop up into a meeting without warning. I did not have a problem with being held accountable for poor performance, though. Do your job. I respect it. The months leading up to this, my highlighted problems were receiving solution-less feedback. I was still meeting 80 percent of my scorecard. I still had the best settlement figures on the team and was the top performer. As a leader, you cannot blindside someone with a write-up without giving them solutions. This was my first and last write-up. It was also my last nine months in this department before I took my career into my own hands.

Everything about how I was treated from my first day told me I would never be taken seriously. After nearly five attempts at moving up, it was clear I would never be anything more than an adjuster. No one believed in me, so I had to believe in myself. I got myself together.

You do what you have to do when your back is against the wall. If they were not going to help me properly, I had to help myself.

I had to set the record straight after they tried to gaslight me. Yes, this was a write-up. No, they did not offer solutions. No, prior to this, there were no real coaching sessions. They wanted me to work within new parameters: First contact on new claims must be made within six hours instead of twenty-four hours (the way it always was previously and the way it currently is today). Despite a lack of sense, it didn't matter. Managers obviously weren't being properly trained. And empathy was nowhere in this conversation.

In saving myself, my solution was simple. I created an email template I could copy and paste to send for new claims. I showed them my plan. They approved it. I took off, and my numbers turned around in one week. In thirty days, I was off their radar again, as I like to stay. Shortly after I was released from the performance action plan, I took short-term disability. I had to reset. I was dealing with serious mental health issues. I was not all right. The trip I took to the crisis center? I was diagnosed with post-traumatic stress disorder. I hit the mental health trifecta: anxiety, depression, and now confirmed PTSD. Pow, right in the kisser. TKO. I have never seen a day in physical warfare, yet, according to science, my brain makeup shows PTSD due to a complexly traumatic childhood, putting me on the same mental playing field as a veteran who has seen actual battle.

At this time, I was only twenty-three. I was estranged from my father's side—and still am. The daddy issues were so very real. I was in contact with my mom, my nana, and my mom's youngest sister. Even during COVID-19, the only time I was included on a Zoom call with other members of my mom's side was when my nana's youngest sister passed away.

There were so many emotions going on inside of me. I felt alone with no one to relate to. A main issue I created for myself was not listening to my partner, which made living with his family a pain for everyone. My world was falling apart, and it was on me.

After about two months on leave, I went back to work right as we were bringing in the new year. I was refreshed. I was renewed. I had something to focus on outside of work. Amid the various suggestions recommended during my weekly therapy sessions, I took on a passion project to help in my moving-through-the-healing process. My therapist said putting something good into the world would naturally help me move through my emotions. As I wrote the scripts for my previously mentioned podcast, I looked at things differently. Talking with guest speakers helped widen my perspective on various things.

When I was not at work, I would be engulfed in research for days. Similar to what I contributed to the podcast at work years later, I created a yearly outline for content ideas. I looked up everything from national holidays to random days people created to celebrate nothing (like National Squirrel Appreciation Day; don't ask me why they need a whole day). It was the first time I realized people everywhere are looking for someone to relate to, someone to celebrate with, someone with whom they can be human. *Empathy is a universal requirement.* I created a long list of weekly affirmations for self-love and empowerment. I wanted to put encouraging words on the airwaves in case someone needed to hear them.

As the year went on, my time at work was all right for a few months. All it took was for me to go on vacation for a week. It was the best week I had had in years: my mom, Nana, and youngest auntie on the road to the Grand Canyon. Being in their presence was beyond refreshing and filled with love. I felt safe and soothed. It was a recentering. Those women are my foundation, and I learned this from taking the trip.

We drove four hours one way. Naturally, I had the aux. There was no other way. I took requests before we packed up the car to create a playlist everyone could enjoy. As we headed down the road, I took a video of the scenery and tried to control my motion sickness.

By the time we arrived, I felt better. We got there right at dusk. We were able to get a few pictures in. On the second day, we went back and got more. On every part of the trail, we were stopped by people who were fascinated by how much we looked alike, and once my nana started providing explanations, she had strangers in awe of how young everyone looked versus the ages she shared with them. I always laugh, like, come on now, everybody knows Black don't crack . . . when you take care of it right.

This brief trip was the perfect source of motivation to redo my résumé and cover letter. I was tired of being rejected. I was tired of the apathy. I was tired of the lack of training and awareness within the management team. I had no immediate plan but knew I wanted it ready. Sure enough, upon my return, I came back to over thirty unreturned voicemails. I cannot say this was done on purpose or if our backup team was too busy to help me, as was the expectation. I can say it certainly was a sign to search the job board immediately.

After searching for less than an hour, I landed on an interim supervisor opportunity in a different department. I kept my attempt to leave close to the chest. I had been blocked from moving up before. I was not chancing anything. I applied on the Monday I returned after my trip, interviewed the following week, had another interview the week after that, and was hired within thirty days. If this is not proof that what is meant for you will happen, I do not know what is. In the span of a year, I went from struggling—experiencing breakdowns, receiving another diagnosis, being written up and stressed out to the point that I had to take leave—to thriving: successfully beating the write-up, returning from leave, resuming my top-performer tendencies, going on my first family girls trip to get my thoughts together, earning my first supervisory role with the company, and buying our first house with my partner; don't call it a comeback. It was a cleanup. A big one.

As we are all young and dumb in our twenties, we all start "young and dumb" and inexperienced in our professional careers. We can always learn from others. This is, in part, why I love having guest speakers on podcasts and in team's huddles. Everybody is an expert in something, and I know my guests know more about a lot of things than me. It is my job to be ready with questions. While they present, it is their show. Listening allows for follow-up questions and natural dialogue. Communication takes practice. With empathy, we want to give others the space to feel their feelings and try to understand them. Positive communication is more than verbal language; it's also body language. In leadership, this is important. If someone is troubled by something, try to understand why. Even if it's a performance issue, respectfully getting to the bottom of it will solve the issue—and help them.

You need every person in your unit to believe you believe in them. Attention to their professional *and* personal well-being is a requirement. Real leaders help develop people from a holistic viewpoint. If you improve the person, you improve the employee.

Empathy contributes to you having an essential leadership quality—emotional intelligence—which contributes to effective leadership, stronger relationships, improved communications, and better decision-making.

The development of empathy and emotional intelligence takes time and energy. Do not be discouraged. Do not rush. Dealing with people's feelings is tricky. Give yourself grace as you learn to work through new scenarios. Utilize your village for guidance and counsel.

Your people will be appreciative. Your leaders will be appreciative. You will later be appreciative for embarking on the learning journey. It will be worth every ounce of effort you put into this, helping you self-authenticate who you are as a leader.

So, how will you lead by example?

Reflect on a moment in which you were denied empathy (directly or indirectly) and the impact. How did you feel? What did you do afterward? How, if at all, did the experience change you?

____

____

____

____

____

____

____

____

____

____

____

____

____

____

____

____

____

HOW TO SECURE YOUR AUTHENTICITY INSURANCE
WITH *Empathy*

Always start personally. Business will always be there.
The people may not be.

*Emotional intelligence is just one key to unlocking our best
selves, together.*

Chapter Eight

Self-care

'm a big believer in the "put your mask on first and then assist someone else" mentality, with emphasis on the "then assist someone else" part. You cannot be authentically you if you are not taking care of you first. And as you take care of yourself, you should take care of others and give back. This could be something large: Perhaps, as you climb in your career, you make it a point to help others improve their interview skills or network to make new connections. Maybe, like me, you have written recommendation letters for people who were affected by job displacement. Or it could be something small, like sharing personally beneficial self-care tips. I've shared my skincare routine with those who've asked. Buttah Skin or Bolden brands work great for melanated skin. Hashtag support Black owned businesses.

Skin routine discussions aside, self-care has become one of my favorite topics over the years, with my appreciation beginning a few years ago, when my training director gave me an assignment for a team summit. There were no set parameters or requirements. I love being given something without guidance because who doesn't like autonomy to trust their instincts? Plus, with this assignment, she was asking me to use my creative, inquisitive spirit to create a segment within our summit for our team to balance work with self. Or at least this is what it turned into.

Self-care was my topic. I immediately discovered, not shockingly, I was not taking proper care of myself. I felt I was missing out on the rest of me, on my needs, yet I never could put words to it to act. It always felt like something was missing. Maybe you feel this way too and are also potentially not caring for yourself as well as you could be. I mean, people speculate that you lose yourself in relationships, not taking some kind of care of yourself first; I found this to be true for myself. I was consumed with *his* state, trying to be in *his* family's good graces, and failing miserably most of the time, per my bull-crashing-around-in-a-china-shop comment some chapters ago. Of course, I wasn't taking good care of *me*.

No one taught me how to "take care of myself" in any particularly defined way, other than to trust in God and He will provide. I also absorbed the message of *go to work, pay bills, live below your means, do not be materialistic, family comes first, be selfless, and help those who need it.* Some good lessons, but not always healthy when you don't understand the need for balance. I was rarely encouraged to look out for myself only, hence why I never knew what a party for me looked like until my high school graduation.

I was consistently called selfish, despite always doing what others asked, even through stone-cold manipulation. I still remember my dad's disapproval when I moved out at eighteen.

Leaving was more an act of self-care to rescue myself than a lesson in it. It was this work project on self-care for the team summit that opened my mind. Oh, how I wish I had known these truths about taking care of me much earlier. I was allowed to worry about myself first? It was unheard of. What was taking care of myself supposed to look like? Why did I feel guilty for even thinking about taking care of myself? Was it my relationship? Was it work? Was it my own self-esteem? Whose voice was playing in my head?

I can tell you the voice is mighty quiet these days. There is nothing ringing in my ear about me doing what I need to do for myself. Not a damn thing. I am not putting myself out for anyone. I am not making myself uncomfortable to fit other people's expectations. Before I consider doing anything, I evaluate the effects of what it means for me and my household. And if it is not good for me, then it is not good for my household.

Once I shared the six areas of self-care for my team at work, it was nearly impossible not to immediately apply the knowledge in every other area and share with anyone who would listen. Truthfully, from this point, I believed it was my responsibility to model self-care, *always*. Over time, it was sad to know most people did not know all six areas either. This made me want to push this message more. We work in a stable and difficult industry. Why not teach people how to take care of themselves? I am not the only working professional who does not know the in-depth meaning of self-care. How many other people are missing out? How many are much older and still unaware?

For you to be successful, you need to look at self-care from a holistic point of view. This means you need to understand how to take care of yourself from a practical, spiritual, physical, mental, emotional, and social perspective. It may seem like a lot, and you may wonder how you are supposed to fit each aspect into your life. Before we go any deeper, remember small wins are still wins. Credit yourself for everything you do. Avoid discouraging self-talk and negative reflections. Avoid the word "should" as much as possible. Self-care is about nurturing you and taking your time. Show yourself grace, patience, and understanding because where else and who else are you going to get it from? Do yourself a favor and create a gratitude board, affirmation board, and vision board. I promise it will all come together.

You know you must survive first. We all got to eat. We all have bills. If you are in a relationship, you have your partner to think about daily. If you have children, they take up a lot of your time. Dwelling on these basic thoughts, this is where practical self-care resides. It looks like meal prepping, doing laundry, even budgeting and managing your finances. Practical self-care is the basic thing you probably already do every day without realizing it.

Cranky because you have not eaten today? Are you worried about when the next bill is due? Are you behind on your household chores? When you think about these things, have you ever noticed the negative shift that happens inside your brain? Do you feel worried? Anxious? Tense? Does it add to your stress level? You are probably neglecting self-care.

Growing up, there was hardly ever food in the house. This was a source of stress, as I always wondered what and when I was going to eat next, at least before my mom started calling my school directly to pay toward my food account. Knowing where your next meal is coming from is as stressful for a child as it is for an adult. It feels worse as an adult because we have a funny way of guilting ourselves when we fall short. Eating ramen for dinner for a whole week is shameful somehow, despite it merely being an act of survival. This is where gratitude comes in. A lot of us are missing the point behind gratitude. Gratitude helps you celebrate the small wins. You go from the mindset of "Ramen again? I am not doing something right" to "At least I know how to turn ramen into real cuisine." Pro tip: Add a protein and use your own spices versus the included spice pack.

I learned how to spice up my ramen from my father. Add eggs or another meat for protein. His favorite seasoning was oregano. I do not know anything he did not put oregano on. I am grateful for the moments in the kitchen where he would show me how to put a meal together out of nothing. This prepared me for later. As an adult, I find myself getting the bare minimum, spending only $100 a week at the grocery store. You could look in our refrigerator and see it empty, whereas I see at least four meals easy because we keep the staples.

Something else he taught me was the importance of spirituality. He was always a God-devoted man. He would put his faith before himself and his own family at times. This did not always suit him in the end; however, if you are going to die on a hill, I guess it is better when you believe you are dying on the hill God meant for you to die on. Everything we did was about pleasing God and making sure we were in his favor. We could not do anything or be with anyone outside of the organization. At times, it seemed like God did not want us to have fun with how our household was set up. God did not want us to explore our natural talents or interests. Our household was a prison. Moving out at eighteen was my jailbreak, except the warden, my father, could not technically stop me, and his wife did not care because her actions year over year showed she never wanted me there anyway. Her whole mood shifted to happiness when she saw I was leaving for real.

Once I was "free," I was not *actually* free. One thing that never left me was the need for spirituality. My poor home experiences did not make me believe there was no God. It did become impossible to pray though. Naturally, my spiritual self-care was in a dark place, and it stayed there because most of the people I came to associate with over the years did not have a religion or go to church. To date, I think only one of my closest friends regularly goes to church with her mother on Sundays. Bless them both. Most knew their family's denomination, but no one was really in a place of worship every week. We hardly ever spoke of God or Jesus or anything related to religion at all. This lack of pressure from my new surroundings made it easy to sink into this dark place spiritually.

Thanks to working on the project for my team's summit, I learned that spiritual self-care was any spirit-nurturing activity pushing you to think in big-picture form. It is anything helping you process deep thought and have something beautifully positive spring forth. You could meditate daily. You could have a dedicated reflection time where you think about the day, what went well, what could have gone better. Break out the gratitude board and affirmation board. You must breathe and speak life into yourself. Stating what you are thankful for every day will allow a gradual shift to more consistent positive thinking. And self-affirmations—*I am powerful, intelligent, determined*—will program you to love yourself to bring out the best version of you.

My partner and I created an all-in-one board in our bedroom. He painted a chalkboard section, and we split it into three sections, with a *T* shape in the middle. The to-do list (our vision board) was on the top, and the gratitude and affirmation boards were on the bottom, one on each side. It was something we always wanted to do, a small feature carrying great long-term benefits. Waking up to our long- and short-term goals, our gratitude and empowering words illuminate a path to where we need to go and what we need to better understand each other—and ourselves.

Having our board visible and in our face every day also contributed to our physical self-care. Physical self-care relates to anything concerning your overall health and well-being. You can do whatever form of exercise you imagine: riding a bike, going for a walk, or running. But are you getting enough sleep at night? How much water do you drink in a day? Does your meal plan regularly include the consumption of fruits and vegetables? Are you taking your vitamins? Do you get outside regularly for natural sunlight and fresh air?

My physical self-care routine took time. I am proud to say I have been consistently exercising for over five years. When we were living with my partner's family, I found a hot yoga studio and went every morning to a 5:30 a.m. or 6:00 a.m. class. Within a year, I was in the best shape I had ever been in. For the first time, my stepmother's voice—"You're not skinny; you need to watch what you eat"—was quieter. When you are body-shamed so young, you really do not know how "healthy" looks or feels. But I was able to see what my body could do, what my body needed, and how my body reacted to stress and new challenges.

During this time, we tried premade deliverable meals. It saved so much time. It was affordable from a financial standpoint too. It made things easy and convenient. And the benefits of the type of meals we received, mainly a meat, vegetables, and a starch (if any), sped up the process of me seeing my body in a more positive image. It boosted my confidence and my health.

Between preprepared meals and hot yoga, I was empowered, feeling in control of my body. I even phased out of asthma. I could control my breathing much better in general. I knew it was possible to grow out of asthma because my older half brother did it. I never knew how he did it though. By the time I was eighteen, he was already married, so I did not witness his progress. As adults, we did not talk much either, so when I did have his attention, I did not waste it. In recent years, my talk of growth has been me telling him, "I am this close"—pressing my index finger and thumb to the point they almost touch—"to having abs." He was always my inspiration for a fit body. The man stayed in the gym. He put me onto hot yoga. Thanks to him, I understand the kind of approach to my physical health that I need to take and have made it part of my regular routine.

Today, I exercise at home. Yoga and Pilates are my go-to, and much like other people, I avoid cardio and the gym. Additionally, in learning from my brother, I recognized that meal prep was the way to go, whether I was good at it or not. I normally have a busy schedule, so taking hours out of any day is very difficult, and meal prepping for a whole week is time-consuming. I accepted my small win of mainly cooking at home. On average, during a good month, we maybe only order out twice. I work from home, which makes it easy to say I have food at home if I am always here. It kind of makes it a requirement.

The most improvement I have had in my body image has been my relationship with food. I was never diagnosed with any eating disorder, but the thought was always in the back of my mind. *Why did I always want more even when I was full? Why could I not get a grip on overeating to avoid suffering the consequences afterward? Why did I feel shame for snacking? Whose voice was this in my brain when I had been taking care of myself for so long?* This was the same voice that would come out when my partner would buy me clothes to wear. Something was saying this outfit does not look right on you, even though he is a professional designer and stylist. Thankfully, he would affirm the work I had done on my body and reassure me due to my petite nature that I would be able to wear things most people could not. This alone would eventually shift my perspective. Never hearing words like these in my entire life, a piece of me still internally cries in disbelief. I am grateful for my partner being a different voice when I needed it most.

We both do well to be sounding boards for each other in taking care of our bodies and mental health. We only get one body and one brain to operate everything. Mental self-care is a little more straightforward, as it represents any stimulating activity. Your mental health needs to be refreshed sometimes, challenged often, and fed consistently. Like how what you put into the world, you get back? What you put into your brain, you get back.

Caring for your mental health looks like reading a book. It could be playing chess with a worthy opponent. (I am not. I think I won maybe one game against my partner the year I bought him a chess set for Father's Day.) I used to be a crossword puzzle person. My nana would always have a crossword puzzle book somewhere. Eventually, I learned sudoku. You get the point; there's plenty to do. My mom's side of the family was very adventurous and loved to learn. We found ourselves visiting museums when we had the opportunity or packing up the car for a road trip to visit a national landmark. Or it could be something simpler, like when my youngest aunt put me onto coloring books.

Your mental and emotional health are similar and often linked. Caring for emotional health looks like participating in an activity that helps you process or reflect on your feelings. It could be a hobby, allowing you to connect with your feelings. While museums may not be for everyone, the National Museum of African American History and Culture had me all the way in my feelings. I took this trip with my mom, which satisfied my emotional and mental needs at the time, loving to learn and simultaneously bonding with a parent. Technically, a combination of emotional, mental, and social self-care.

Under regular circumstances, how would you set aside time to understand your daily emotions? How would you express your daily emotions? Examples to try out could be playing a musical instrument or listening to music. I love journaling and encourage you to start. You can try out your hand at journaling via *The Authentic Leader Journal.* One question per day and no set time frame. Just one year of dedicating time to you for you to see what changes happen in your life. It really does make all the difference when you see your words in front of you versus only hearing them in your head and feeling them in your heart. Writing things down makes it real, and sometimes we all need a little reprogramming.

If you are a visual artist, you could draw or paint or sculpt or do anything with your hands to create something beautiful. You could love knitting, sewing, and crocheting. You could love gardening and having the best view in the entire neighborhood. You could enjoy watching your favorite show or movie in solitude. Sometimes the right song, movie, or show can say everything you can't say in real life, and putting it on can feel reaffirming to you. If this leads you to feelings of anger, sadness, disappointment, resentment, or other negative things, do not run from your feelings. The bigger the feelings, the more you sink deeper into your activity for natural self-soothing. For me, putting a song on repeat (sometimes for days) has been enough to self-soothe me through some big feelings.

We are humans. Feelings of all kinds are natural, and we must embrace them, learn to control them. While a feelings wheel might seem childish to you, it teaches adults to go beyond the normal "happy," "sad," and "mad." Emotions are complex. Labeling them helps us work through them. Getting a grip on feelings personally avoids bringing baggage to work.

Bringing your baggage into work makes it easy for people to formulate negative opinions about you. Take control of your narrative by watching what you say, how you say it, and facial expressions. Before you hit send on an email, reread your message a million times.

Identifying your feelings avoids sending a nastygram to someone who meant no harm in the first place.

Controlling your emotions and feelings to better control your narrative will in turn help you have better control on your social interactions overall. Social self-care is the final type we will discuss. Social self-care in its simplest form has to do with how you strengthen your relationships with the people you have in your village. How deep is your love? How strong is your bond with the people you care about? What does a healthy relationship or friendship look like to you? What can you do to grow closer to another person?

Go back to the basics. Start a conversation with a friend to see how they are doing and if they are okay. Ask about interests, jobs, hobbies, plans, goals, pop culture. The list goes on. Social self-care prioritizes bonding with your people. Share a meal at your home, their home, or a restaurant. Go to the movies. Go bowling. Go horseback riding. Travel. Go to the beach. Listen to an audiobook together. Have a book club. Go shopping. Play basketball or another sport together. Sketch, paint, or just talk.

I make it part of my routine to FaceTime my nana. She tells me how she and my aunt are doing and their plans for the week or month. Talking to her about my endeavors every week inspires me.

Social self-care also allows you to practice empathy and emotional intelligence. Regular human interaction will nurture others as much as it nurtures you. Eventually, when you have your routine down and you are regularly communicating with all those in your village, you will feel such ease. No conversation is forced or rushed. Everything flows. You feel . . . happy. Indulging in self-care will make you happy. Indulging in self-care will help you improve as a person. By giving yourself permission to put you first, you will then be able to show up for others. Do not let anyone make you feel bad or inferior or less than because you chose you. People will act as if you have changed so much. And you know what? Tell them yes, you have. Tell them you are proud of finally figuring out what was missing in your life. You. You were what was missing.

As it relates to social self-care, I will not be the first nor the last to tell you protecting yourself is always top priority. People will not understand what you mean or what you need to do for yourself. This is okay. Self-care is not for others, though they may benefit on the back end. Self-care is for you. It is okay to set boundaries with one-way streeters. You are valuable. As is your time and energy. You deserve reciprocation.

In the decade I have been estranged from my father's side of the family, I have attempted to make amends on several occasions. Yes, you read correctly. It is what my late grandmother would have wanted, for there to be peace and connectivity, not division. Plus, the way I see it, we are all still family. I do not want to get a phone call saying my father was found dead alone in his home. And I wish no ill on my stepmother or her children. Did I appreciate my experience living with them? No. Do I appreciate the person I am today because of living with them? Yes. We talked about love being forgiveness and how everyone needs forgiveness. I thought if I told them I forgive them, maybe things would begin to improve.

The first attempt was with my father in the first year I lived in my first apartment. I invited him over. I had no knowledge that he was bringing his wife, and she had the audacity to bring one of the congregation's young children, still playing in my face. I was *hot*, feeling disrespected in my own home, and literally could have punched her in her face. Thankfully, she and the young child did not stay long. If memory serves me correctly, he asked them to wait in the car after a few minutes. From there, he and I had a conversation that ended in him walking away from me because he did not like how I was calling him and his wife out for the things they did and literally *just did*, triggering still fresh wounds of how much she cared for every other child around her and treated me like absolute dog shit. I may have been disrespectful, and for this I apologized years later the next time I saw him. You read correctly again. I did not hear from him again after the incident at my first apartment for years. It was complete radio silence. Not a text or call. He randomly wrote me a letter when we lived with my partner's family. And I was heated because I never gave him my address, and it felt like a total invasion of my privacy. If I wanted you to know where I was, you would know.

A few years after the visit to my first apartment but before my partner and I moved in with his family, my younger brother ran into my partner at the mall. This prompted a text message. A text message turned into a meal at the Cheesecake Factory. How much he had grown since I last saw him at my grandmother Lee's funeral in 2015. His body physically changed. He was taller, with more facial hair. But his mind seemed almost the same as when we were still living as teenagers together. We talked for a couple hours. I explained some of the things his mother did, of which he allegedly had no knowledge. It was clear when we were younger, we had completely different experiences. It was even clearer that he was just now realizing this was the truth himself. Part of him was still in denial, even though he was usually right there for all of it. Perception and reality really are two different things.

Though it was not his place to apologize for his mother's actions, I do remember he was sorry. I could tell he felt bad. I could tell this was probably one of the first real conversations he had with someone in his adult life. Remember, I am only ten months his senior. Keep in mind, this was also the first real conversation he and I ever had about anything. I have not sugarcoated anything yet, so I will not start now. He was a piece of work as a younger brother. He was a slob—naturally, boys are usually gross. He was always in trouble, which means I was always feeling the residual effects. His mother hated that I never really did anything bad (grades or behavior) like her children seemed to do on the regular in school, which did not make things easy. Once he got to high school, I loved the thought of having a sibling with me. I loved telling people he was my brother and not to mess with him or telling my friends if they saw somebody messing with him to let me know. I had a strong enough reputation at school where I had zero problems stepping up if he needed me. We just never had a close relationship. It was no one's fault then. We were kids.

As adults, I will one-hundred-percent blame religion. I suppose there is a lack of diversity everywhere. This part of my family allowed the interpretation by men who did not write the Bible or know the initial intentions to come between us having a healthy relationship. Some, if you ask, will say they are keeping themselves clean. Clean from what? Am I unclean because I do not attend the Kingdom Hall? Yet, I am not too unclean for him to ask me if my partner can set him up with a suit for his wedding the month before the date. A wedding of which I had zero knowledge. I was sent a blurry video and photos to let me know he was engaged. I could barely see her face. And my questions to try to learn more about her were ignored. I am not good enough to be treated like family, but when you need something, you feel comfortable enough to call? I think not. I did try after this at least once or twice. I remember inviting him to our house once we bought it because we lived fifteen minutes away from each other. None of my invitations were ever accepted. Radio silence there now too. Two people down, one more to go.

A few years later, I was out walking at a park with a friend who just had a baby. We were doing our thing, making laps. I was pushing the stroller, and we were chatting away. Randomly, I heard a familiar voice without seeing the face yet. For some reason, their dogs caught my attention first. Then, my eyes raised to their faces. And BAM! There she was, in her four-foot-eleven glory: my stepmother. I had not seen her since my grandmother's funeral. Many emotions rushed over me. I told my friend I would catch up with her and the baby at the car. When my friend walked away, seeing my stepmother's face again made me angry and sad at the same time. Would you believe me if I told you I apologized to her? It was a shock when the words left my lips too. I believed at the time that I could at least apologize for any hardship I caused her and my father's relationship, to which she let me know they were separated, and things were not all my fault.

When we hugged, I think I was still crying, but I cannot tell you if it was because I was releasing all the feelings I had built inside me or if it was painful to restrain myself from snapping her like a twig. Thank goodness I was raised a Witness and violence is not within my nature.

After this encounter, I thought I was ready to talk. My triggers reminded me that I wasn't, and I quickly realized that I was not ready to speak on any cordial level. Then, there was the thought that if she and my father were separated, why would our relationship be necessary? He and I may not have been on speaking terms, but I will always be for my family. I did not trust her. Anyone who can abuse a child is untrustworthy to me. I could not be around her because I would never know her real intentions. She smiled in my face before. I will never make the mistake of believing her ever again.

Fast-forward another year and some change. I attempted to reconnect with her and my father on my own terms when I thought I was ready. I sent them both voice messages via text to apologize and offer truce. Both accepted. However, the one with her did not last very long after I found out the truth about their separation: She had filed for divorce. She left this part out during our park reunion. Again, this is why she is untrustworthy. You let me cry in your face and withheld the most important detail of all that you literally left him as COVID-19 was happening and he had been struggling ever since. It wasn't surprising though. She was not here to be a parent or a partner. I thought, when you get married, the vow is for richer or for poorer. I suppose not.

In attempting to reconnect with my father after sending that message, I learned a lot about what really happened from his perspective, more than I care to know. And it filled in a lot of blanks (not all had to be filled). If anything, it affirmed many things for me, the main one being that they were not a fit from the beginning, and neither of them wanted to admit it. He could not see past his loneliness. She could not see past her own desires. I feel sorry for them both. I wish I could say he and I were in a better place; however, we still have radio silence. I sent them both text messages, letting them know I would indefinitely be taking space from them. For the sake of my own health and growth, I had to step back all the way. All the way looked like blocking their numbers and completely switching the type of phone I used, going from being an iPhone user of ten years to a Google Pixel 7 Pro. The change was very symbolic for me, and it did wonders for my health. I hope he has taken the time apart to reflect so we may reconnect when it is safe to do so for both of us. I do believe time heals all things.

Time (and effort) can heal you too, so take your time and take care of you. I cannot put it any other way: Self-care is so important for us as humans first, professionals second. I was missing so much of what I needed to really do the work to begin my healing. At times, I allowed my unhealed self to affect me in the workplace and with my relationships outside of work. You do not have to be this way. You can have healthy relationships. You can reduce your stress levels and minimize the burnout effect imposed by heavy workloads and tight project deadlines. You can be happier. You can be healthier. You can have some of the best relationships you have ever had in your life, relationships you want to hold onto for better or for worse. You can accomplish the unbelievable and the incredible. There is no reason why we should not be making self-care our number-one priority.

So, what will you do to ensure your needs are met?

What are you neglecting about yourself? How can you adopt
a healthy self-care routine?

HOW TO SECURE YOUR AUTHENTICITY INSURANCE
WITH *Self-care*

Execute at least one practice per type of self-care every day for a full thirty days. Repeat!

You cannot help anyone before yourself, and you cannot help yourself if you do not get out of your own way.

Chapter Nine

Leadership

Do you imagine yourself being a leader in the future? Why or why not? What would you hope to accomplish? Who would you want to help? What problem(s) would you want to solve? How would you inspire a team? What would be your approach to communication? What do you think your biggest challenge(s) would be? How are you with conflict? Would you push for diversity, equity, and inclusion to be part of every aspect in the workplace? Do you have any innovative ideas you would implement to improve your internal employee(s) as well as your external customer experience?

For those already overseeing a team, why did you want to be a leader? Did you intentionally apply knowing this was the next thing you wanted to do, or did someone hand you the opportunity? Were you ready to lead others? Are you concerned about your team's well-being? What is your relationship with each of your team members? How are you with pushback and conflict? Are you open to feedback? Can people readily approach you? If someone were asked for an opinion of you, what do you believe would be said about you? What happens if someone underperforms? How do you handle it?

Possessing the quality of leadership means you can influence other people on an individual, team, organization, or even country level. With this definition, leadership also indicates you must be able to get people to move in a certain direction. You notice anything else about leadership's definition? There is nothing about the word leadership requiring you to carry a title of power. You can be no one and still be a leader if you are able to guide people to make positive decisions. Leadership is complicated when we make it complicated. Let's uncomplicate it by flushing out everything leadership is *not* so we can get to what leadership *is*.

You do not have to be working toward a role in leadership or seeking it for an opportunity to fall in your lap. Life happens this way at times. As stated earlier, if you stay ready, you do not have to get ready. It applies to everything, everywhere, all the time. Imagine being given the green light to do something you have been waiting your turn to try. Why would you not want to take off immediately? Green means "go" for a reason. You *go*!

In reflecting on my own questions at the outset, I believed myself to be a leader before I carried the title. Always the youngest in the room, I never wanted to stand out. I did my best to blend in. I even took my partner's advice and changed how I dressed to appear more mature. Who knew adding heels to anything would instantly create a "mature" persona?

Continuing my reflection, I knew I wanted to help people like me who were overlooked and underwhelmed with growth opportunities. I wanted to contribute to the solutions needed for diversity, equity, and inclusion to feel real at work. I wanted to inspire my colleagues to do excellent work and to be willing to help one another. I considered my approach to communication one with care because I wanted to give others the experience I did not have personally. I did not feel included at all, nor did I feel equal, and nor was there any real diversity until I was in the driver's seat and elevated to a leadership title. I knew one of my biggest challenges was going to be developing my ability to be empathetic. I had zero clue that my biggest challenge would be an employee calling me racist in a survey. The toll this took was as you can imagine: rough.

I am proud to say now that I handle conflict *way* better than I did ten years ago. Keeping my cool, keeping level. Way back, I went toe to toe with an employee in front of my leader. And when a similar situation happened later down the line, I let the employee speak and calmly showed receipts and evidence in a dignified manner to disprove their statements. My manager called after to say there was a night-and-day difference.

For many obvious reasons, I wanted to fight the fine fight for diversity, equity, and inclusion to be part of every aspect in the workplace. I wanted to help bridge the generational gap and the race gap where possible. Most of the ideas I have are directly related to improving the employee experience, which begins with ensuring all the leaders have been trained the same. I cannot tell you how much I hear about onboarding being a garbage experience in various industries. To me, it all comes down to one thing. How is the leadership set up? How did the people in leadership get there in the first place?

You have people who earned it, worked, scraped, bled to the bone. You have others who knew a person who got them in, not necessarily on real skill, talent, or experience. No matter how you enter leadership, you have one agenda. Your people must always come first. Your people must always be taken care of before you. It is your job to ensure they never go without. And if there is a time where you are the one holding them back, own up, communicate, and apologize; then follow through.

I wanted to be a leader because I believed I was ready to lead others. I could execute objectives while equally being concerned about the bottom line, as I am about each individual team member's well-being. I aimed to make every relationship with each person on a team unique. Each relationship is special and dependent upon how open the person is to being open with me. I never push anyone past a certain comfort point in conversation. I go as far as they go. I also remain open to feedback to the point of including it as my closing statement for every email: "Please feel free to reach out with any questions, concerns, or feedback." And that went just before my previous "You are light. Be light" mantra above my name in the signature. Now it's "Have & Show gratitude."

I do not mind pushback. I am known to push back myself. Ask my partner. My people can approach me and be received well, pending their approach. You can tell me you disagree without being disrespectful or mean. If someone talked to anyone who has reported to me, they would say all these things and more. I was able to foster genuine friendships upon departing a previous leadership role, and I have no doubt I will keep the lines open with my current team should our team roster ever change. I believe they would say my energy is genuine, my positivity infectious, and I am very straightforward. If someone underperforms, it is only a conversation. It is not a scolding or a reprimanding. I am no one's parent.

Underperformers are underperforming because (1) they do not like what they do, (2) they are not good at what they do, possibly because they were not given the right tools or training to carry the right understanding, (3) they do not like their leader, or (4) they do not care because no one has impressed upon them why they should care. The way I look at an underperformer is not disdainful. As leaders, sure, we will become upset when employees underperform. However, to not help them get better—or worse, to hold a grudge—is counterproductive and childish. As one of my previous leaders stated, it is your job to either "coach up or coach out." Ultimately, you choose.

A human first, employee second approach has always worked best for me. I will take the time to ask how things are going at work and at home. I will share my observations of their disposition and demeanor if I notice their body language is off during a group session. Open-ended questions can do the trick, especially when you sound as if you care. It does not take much to sound as if you care. "What's going on with you? Anything new? I noticed you were less active in our huddle today. Is there anything I can do to help?"

With this approach, I have been informed of deaths, divorces, issues with kids, parental health issues, spousal health issues, personal health issues, you name it. This approach is gentle, sincere, to the point. It says, "I pay attention to you. I notice when you are not yourself. Are you okay? Is there anything you want me to know? Do you need my help in any way? Whatever your problem, personal or work, I am here to listen if this is what you need." People do feel when you care about them. It is not something you can fake or dismiss.

The next generation is not tolerating being dismissed for the sake of a paycheck. Post COVID-19, people everywhere had epiphanies about their personal health and well-being, which makes sense because, at one point, I'm sure we all thought we were going to die. It was the scariest time I have ever seen in my short life. They say these types of events happen at least once a century, and I am grateful, hopefully, we are done for a while, and if you are alive now, likely you will not be the next go-round.

If anything, COVID-19 also initiated the era of people working for themselves as quickly as they could download the rideshare and food delivery apps. It is very serious. You cannot shirk being a real leader anymore if you want people to help you drive your company's mission. You cannot be in leadership for the wrong reasons anymore. Legacy leaders need to get past old-fashioned ways and adapt to the present.

We need leaders with vision who can plan, strategize, and execute. We need leaders who can give and receive feedback and are unafraid of not being the smartest person in the room. Leaders need the voice of the people to know how to lead them. Every team is different, and the cookie-cutter approach will not work. Taking in the opinion of your people, whether you have an entire strategy mapped out or not, is what will draw your team closer together. One of the best compliments you can give to someone is asking them what or how they think.

You could see a change in a person by sharing the bigger picture with them from the beginning instead of showing end results. There are situations where this is appropriate. And if your team is doing well, meeting or exceeding expectations, you could use the opinion approach to create a development opportunity. If you are in a group setting, you can turn this into a strategy session. Your people can now say they have experience with strategy and planning for new initiatives.

Giving your team more skills to work with and helping them level up is certainly one way to motivate and inspire. Motivating and inspiring your team is near the top of your priorities because if you are unable to motivate and inspire, you likely do not have as much influence as you think you do, at least not genuine influence. Sure, you can get people to act when they are afraid of you, but this is not a genuine influence. This is "I do not want to lose my job, so I am going to do what is asked of me." The person doing something because they do not want to lose their job versus the person doing something because you inspired them to be better at their job will not view you the same way. One person respects your position only. The other respects you as a person based on how you showed up for them and your genuine interest in wanting to see them be great.

A holistically empowered team can reach their full potential. Teams unlocking their full potential usually have a good leader in place, helping to improve communication. We talked about being transparent and as crystal clear as possible. Your open-ended communication will solidify everyone's place or purpose. When everyone understands what they are supposed to be doing, your job as the leader becomes easier. When people understand their role and can manage their day without you, this leaves you all the open time you need to accomplish your own duties.

With more time back to you, you can become more effective with decision-making for yourself and your people. Whether experiencing heavy pressure from a customer escalation or a generally complex challenge, you will face it head-on in the spirit of "come at me, bro." Your ability to assess risk will improve. The stronger and faster you are at weighing pros versus cons in any situation will mean you will be better able to take the right course of action.

Problem-solving is a transferable skill and required even if you never become a manager. A strong leader can self-discover their problems and do something about it without their leader having to step in. A leader who can model the ability to problem-solve for a team will forge a strong bond within that team. It is our responsibility as leaders to build cohesive and collaborative teams. Place a problem in front of your team in a group setting, and instead of giving your ideas first, go around the room instead. See everyone's view. Then go back around the room and see how they would solve it themselves. You may get different ideas. You may get the same ideas. There is not necessarily anything wrong with everyone coming to the same conclusion. In fact, at times, this is exactly what you need to be sure the decision you are about to make is a good one.

The more you make employees feel included, the more inclined they are to self-discover and want to develop. This requires a leader who is truly invested in their people. You must create training opportunities for improvement in their current role and expansion to other roles. You must prove you are in support of their development. One way you can do this is by connecting your team to new people. You must allow and create space for mentorship to happen. They need people outside of you to talk to for consistent coaching. Having a solid manager *and* a solid mentor can pay off greatly for anyone. Assisting your employees by helping them gain new skills and making new relationships is exactly what hungry employees need to advance their careers. Everyone is hungry (unless you are borderline retired, then I understand); some people just do not know it yet, because no one has shown them direct, genuine interest.

This leads me to accountability. A strong leader allows their team to call them out. I expect them to tell me when I have done something wrong or caused offense. If they are not able to hold me accountable, why would I expect them to allow me to hold them accountable? We must make these leader-employee relationships feel like a safe space in more ways than one. If we are going to be holding people accountable for their performance and counting negative metrics against them, then we would be no less than a hypocrite if we were not held at least to the standard of helping them stay on track, which means giving proper warning before a trend turns a pattern and a pattern turns into a problem. And that problem turns into a write-up or termination.

Showing you are adaptable can certainly do wonders for your team's view of you. What happens to you when it is time for change? With so many technological advancements occurring every day all around the world, there is not an industry unaffected, which means there is no one in the world who is not experiencing some kind of change right now. When you think about it, can you feel your heart sink a bit? Really. Think about it. How many people right now at this very moment, out of over eight billion people, are undergoing some kind of change? At home. At work. Internally. All of the above. Imagine, an entire world full of scared humans unsure of what is next.

This is where leaders come in. Leaders are no less fearful of the future. Leaders are leaders because we take things head-on and pave the way for others to be less afraid. Leaders are not afraid to be the first one to try something because failure does not keep us from trying until we reach our desired outcome. Leaders have the ultimate responsibility in modeling how to be adaptable. You are the one your people are experiencing the change through. Your response signals to your team how well you believe you can handle this new thing, and it has a great impact on how they respond to change. If you show fear, your team will be afraid. If you stay calm and composed, your team will see your confidence.

People around you seeing you confidently stride through change with a smile notice someone handling change gracefully. You may not think this a big deal, but it is. You will be inspiring people to also handle change gracefully. You will inspire confidence in people to trust to not lose their heads right away before they hear the major details. Personally, if I do not have all the details, I would prefer to wait to share announcements until I have what I need to be able to properly communicate the message.

Do you show irritation or annoyance? Sometimes yes. Certain opportunities to commiserate with your team may arise. Use discernment. Most of the time, you will want to do your best to apologize and acknowledge everyone's thoughts or feelings so they may see your sincerity for wanting to understand the frustration of change. However, when a team senses you are a boss who is not emotionally intelligent enough to recognize when they are inconvenienced, you may not foster the most positive space.

Creating positive spaces is at the number-one spot on this leadership list of priorities. It is our duty to ensure everyone can feel safe at work. People who believe they are in a positive and supportive workspace feel and perform better and will be less likely to want to quit. It is our duty as leaders to make people want to come to work daily by giving them something to look forward to. No one is saying buy them lunch every day or anything rash. I meet with my folks individually twice per month in addition to one weekly group call. For individual conversations, though, this equates to 24 times per year out of 260 days worked, if they never miss a day and only work on weekdays. In twenty-four sessions, you can change someone's entire outlook on themselves and their career.

Why make your employees feel good when you can make them feel exceptional? You can make anyone feel exceptional, manager title or not. Remember, a leader is anyone with influence. You could not be a leader but utilize these skills as part of a supporting role in an ERG. Or maybe you do community work on your own or support a cause about which you feel strongly.

Speaking in terms of adulthood and relationships, these qualities would do well if we were willing to put in the work on ourselves. What kind of things can you do for yourself and for others when you are feeling inspired? How much better will you be able to express yourself and properly articulate any point to any audience? How will your decision-making evolve from a personal standpoint? Is it possible you will feel more empowered to make choices on a dime because you can easily identify worst- and best-case scenarios? What kind of decisions will you make when your household is a well-oiled machine? There will be no problem you and/or your significant other cannot handle together. You will have a strong sense of team, whether it is just partner and partner or partner and partner plus children or other extended family.

Development is a universal human need. We must keep developing ourselves from a personal standpoint as much as we are developing our professional selves. You can possess all the wonderful talents to accomplish the job, but a crappy attitude will always shine through. Take the time to develop your personality so it attracts as many as possible. You will save yourself from being frustrated with other difficult personalities because you know you worked on you, and the best version of you is present.

The best version of you is accountable. In my personal relationship, accountability has not been a strong suit. Family structures especially will never be successful without accountability and adaptability. We have experienced curveball after curveball. What has helped is how we both possess the ability to be good leaders in our own respective ways. We choose to work on ourselves individually and on our relationship together, as well as plan for the future. We aim to make our environment positive by communicating more, choosing our circles wisely, and setting our goals even more cautiously. Our outlook is always this: How can both our families not have to be stressed in the future?

I kid you not, for the first few years, he lost at least one family member per year due to illness. I lost family as well. We have both worked in hospital settings, and all we think about is how much neither of us wants our mothers to have to be in any kind of facility in their old age. These places are dirty and cold, and the workers are often underappreciated, making inconsistent care an absolutely real thing. Knowing, as leaders, our core values match, and family and legacy over everything, provides me great reassurance. Funny, in just the few days prior to writing this, I found out my great-grandma Bertha Mae (my nana's mother) was twelve years and six months younger than my great-grandpa Harry, the same age difference as me and my partner.

You cannot tell me the universe is not at work on me, honey. Everything that happened in 2024, whether good or bad, showed me exactly what I needed to see in my future. It is bright. It will be prosperous. May yours be as well. You have the power. You have the controls. And if you made it this far into this book, hopefully you have picked up a few new ideas and/or skills.

So, how will you choose to lead?

Explain your leadership style along with three strengths and three weaknesses.

____

____

____

____

____

____

____

____

____

____

____

____

____

____

____

____

____

____

HOW TO SECURE YOUR AUTHENTICITY INSURANCE
WITH *Leadership*

Be a firm role model in your own development, and
others will follow your example.

*A team is only as effective and open as their leader, and a
real leader is open to learning something new.*

Chapter Ten

Endurance

Wow, can you believe you made it to the end? I am extremely grateful that you took your valuable time to listen to me on my soapbox. It took four weeks to put this all together. I somehow managed to write for ninety hours despite a full-time job, a part-time job, and sharing the responsibility of running a household. You could say it was one of my more manic periods, probably one of my longest. How fulfilled and rewarded I feel. I cannot wait to do another! This was the best thirty days of inspiration I have ever had in my entire life. I hope what you have read sparks a fire in you to want to make a difference, whether in your own life or touching someone else.

Whether you are working on you and/or assisting someone else, you are part of a bigger movement, a movement pushing people to want to take control of their lives and their futures, pushing for diversity, equity, and inclusion to be a *real* thing in the workplace, pushing for legacy leaders and the next generation to be of service to one another.

Until we have at least those last two things, the workplace will never really feel safe for anyone. There will always be this tension, this paranoia, this underlying feeling you must watch your back or look over your shoulder. Who wants to feel this way at work or in real life? No one. We as human beings need to shift to the mindset of other human beings assuming good intent so we may allow ourselves to relax. If we work together, we can accomplish anything.

For these reasons, we must endure. We must not quit because we are not getting immediate results. We should not quit because haters are loud and fill the room with their noise. We must not back down from doing what is right. We should all be looking at the bigger picture together because a whole bunch of big-picture ideas make way for big-picture solutions, which leads straight up the stairway to big-picture change. We need it, and we need it sooner rather than later.

What is "endurance"? Merriam-Webster's definition is the ability to withstand hardship or adversity. Hopefully, you do not have to withstand for too long, but it does build your suit of armor. Every test, trial, or tribulation makes you stronger. You can work through stress better, view setbacks and challenges as temporary, and reprogram your brain.

What is the point of setting a goal if you are not going to finish it right? You took the time to make the goal, lay out a plan, and daydream about possible best-case scenarios and panic over worst-case scenarios. Endurance is what pushes you to stay locked in. You will stay committed to short-term and long-term goals. When you can stay on task and execute your own plans, you will be able to accomplish more.

A concept I thought was interesting is how conquering an obstacle and continuing onto your goal can build a person's self-confidence. When you experience difficult situations and make it through to the other side, you believe in your own personal capabilities more because you can do what you may have initially thought to be impossible. We all need to reinforce our mental fortitude. Why not be in control of it? How do you improve your mental toughness? You endure. If athletes train physically to build their endurance to be the best in their sport, why would we not have to build endurance to be the best at work or in life?

Having the capacity to endure means we handle stress and anxiety differently. Hopefully, you will also improve in managing your emotions. There are a few reasons why many shy away from talking about feelings. People can be embarrassed or afraid to feel. They may have been scarred from a previous experience. Again, with the vast number of emotions a person can be consumed with at one time, depending on the situation, it can be overwhelming. Then, you can feel embarrassed about being overwhelmed. Kind of an interesting cycle, but it is a manageable one. You are capable of talking about your feelings freely, with zero restrictions or worries or cares.

Another great way to help you endure, by allowing you the time to sharpen your mind and practice a little introspection, is to get moving. That is right: exercise. Get up and go! Stop making excuses and make it happen. Building physical endurance by exercising while you simultaneously are building your mental fortitude is one of the most strategic things you will ever do. Not only are you catering to the need for you to better your brain and ultimately your nervous system, but you are also improving your physical well-being and stamina in general.

With a strong mind and a strong body, you will be unstoppable, undeniable, undefeatable. When you have more energy because you are not weighed down by mental stress and/or lacking the physical stamina, you are increasing the number of things you will be able to accomplish. Your productivity goes way up! Your work performance will follow. This will give you the sense of accomplishment anyone needs to keep going. If you spend years working toward something and never experience any wins, how discouraged would this leave you? We all need to feel as if progress is being made; otherwise, what is the point? Never feeling satisfied, never feeling like you get anything done. Who *wants* to feel this way? When you feel accomplished in any way, you naturally feel happier.

A happier you makes for a happier and stronger village. Practicing the art of endurance will give you the skills you need to work through conflict resolution with peers, employees, leaders, friends, family, and significant others. How you handle your interactions with others will depend on how happy you are in general. A happy you can bond with others without weight or anxiety or fear. A you capable of bonding is in for much stronger relationships. As the years continue, your village will need to strengthen along with you, so what you do and who you choose to keep in your village matters greatly. You are only as strong as your weakest relationship. So if you need to make some tough decisions, do not feel bad. You are not alone. We all must decide at one point or another who we keep close and who we keep closer. You need people around who are going to be an enriching sounding board to you.

By cultivating an endurance mindset, you will find yourself adapting, possessing a growth mindset more naturally, and be more open to learning throughout your life. Your village must help you endure, not make it harder. Your village strengthens you. It is your place to find motivation and to be inspired in as little as one coffee chat or in-person exchange or phone call. Your village is your place to sharpen the sword of your endurance so you may have a fighting chance at hitting your mark.

Personally, I will never have only one mark. I am a firm believer that you should not put all your eggs in one basket. You should try to diversify your time among the important things in your life and at work. For example, while I work nonstop for paying employers, I have also taken the time to do side projects where I can explore my passions. Use your passions to keep you busy and always be working on you. In trying this approach to overall life productivity, you will find yourself growing at a rapid pace and aligning with your purpose in a more organic and holistic way.

One-hundred-percent self-alignment is a beautiful state to be in, even if only for a brief moment in time. I am coming up on my Saturn cycle soon enough. Maybe then will be my time. But no leader can have a successful time overseeing any number of people without having alignment somewhere. Everyone has not experienced one-hundred-percent self-alignment; however, you do not have to be in perfect alignment to be a leader. Stop waiting for some special moment to happen and take charge of your environment today.

Leaders, if we do not endure, do you know how much longer, if even still feasible, it would take for us to bridge the generational gap in the workplace? All our precious time and effort up to this point would be a waste. Without bigger and better ideas from older and younger generations coming together, companies could stay stagnant in their culture. A company with a stagnant culture risks employee dissatisfaction and higher turnover. If employees do not stay long enough to help fix problems, there is risk to the company's bottom line. There could be more frequent communication breakdowns and employees having low morale. Low morale plus communication breakdown equals trouble.

To keep yourself from being a disgruntled and unmotivated employee, and to help prevent others from falling into this mindset, start with you. Building your endurance looks like what we have talked about throughout this entire book. You must take care of yourself first because self-care is and always will be a priority for your survival. If you are incapable of taking care of yourself, you will never be able to help anyone. Maintaining self makes it possible for you to stay alert, abreast, and active in this journey we are on.

Be sure to show yourself appreciation and affirm your abilities. No one else can do this for you. Show yourself gratitude and love. Encourage others both in and outside of your village to do the same. You never know when an ally will come in handy or what you could learn. We need all the understanding we can get from one another.

We need to be able to celebrate the small wins and the large wins, *all* wins. Guess what? Making progress *is* a small win. At least you were not in the same place as you were before. You moved. Now your hike is slightly shorter than it was previously. You may not be "almost there," but you are "getting there." Getting there is a big deal and should be celebrated joyfully. All it really takes is for you to maintain your momentum and motivation. Endurance will get you to the finish line. You will have such a positive impact by remaining optimistic.

Being optimistic fits right in with maintaining a growth mindset. We need role models who are going to lead by example when it comes to displaying optimism and a growth mindset. We need role models who are persistent and don't accept "no" for an answer, who exhibit patience as we explore new things, new ideas, new processes. There is a point where we do have to say "no," and this is pertaining to when we are on the brink of burnout. Having a strong work ethic is not determined by how much earned time off you leave in the PTO bank. Never feel bad about taking time off from work. Never feel bad about taking your breaks. By law, those are owed to you. Take every minute you can and feel no shame. Stepping away to compose ourselves is how we maintain. We must preserve ourselves. This is part of endurance too.

If I did not endure, who knows what would have been in store.

If I did not endure, I would not know the difference between living within your means and living as if you are poor.

If I did not endure, my passions would have escaped me, lost in the storm.

If I did not endure, I would not know what it means to positively be in rare form.

If I did not endure, all of which my family suffered would be for nothing.

If I did not endure, anything inconvenient would result in me crumbling.

If I did not endure, opportunity after opportunity would pass me by.

If I did not endure, I would not be any closer to finding my "why."

If I did not endure, there would be no space left in my brain.

If I did not endure, I would not know how to differentiate my pain.

If I did not endure, my village would cease to grow.

If I did not endure, all my weaknesses would continue to show.
If I did not endure, there would be no proof I can do anything to which I set my mind.
If I did not endure, I would have never learned how careful to be with my time.
If I did not endure, there would be less improvement and more problems.
If I did not endure, I might have ended up running with the wild ones.

If we do not endure, we risk our entire future because we were tired.
If we do not endure, we will leave entire generations uninspired.
If we do not endure, we could see our lights dimming gradually.
If we do not endure, soon we will be unable to see.
If we do not endure, we miss out on the long-term benefits.
If we do not endure, there will be no one to model true commitment.
If we do not endure, unconscious bias will remain unaddressed.
If we do not endure, microaggressions will continue putting us to the test.
If we do not endure, the path to full connectivity will be lost.
If we do not endure, the price to pay will be a hefty cost.
If we do not endure, the advancements we need to make will never come to fruition.
If we do not endure, we will be unable to make solid decisions.
If we do not endure, trust will be off the table completely.
If we do not endure, there goes our cultural competencies.
If we do not endure, we will never understand one another.
If we do not endure, we will continue making enemies out of our own brothers.

If we do not endure, history will keep repeating itself.

If we do not endure, perhaps none of us will see our intended wealth.

If we do not endure, blessings in abundance could be blocked.

If we do not endure, our mindsets will forever stay locked.

If we do not endure, freedom will always be out of reach.

If we do not endure, you will allow haters to drain you like a leech.

If we do not endure the most authentic version of ourselves, we will never meet.

Connecting all the dots between how we can build our own endurance and what happens when we do not hopefully opens your mind to the big picture. We are in pressing times where your authenticity is a requirement when you have nothing else. It is only through your authenticity that you will be able to withstand and stand out among the rest. There will always be someone who has more skill than you. Remember, technical skills can be taught, while the unique talents you bring, only you possess.

Authentic endurance is crucial in the long-term commitment that comes with successfully building connections and sustaining relationships. It takes time for people to be open to hearing about the various biases existing in the workplace, and even longer to get in gear to do something about it. While you are patiently waiting, you may come across opportunities where you can multitask and have your hand in multiple things simultaneously. A little bit of progress in many areas now equals big change later.

If there is nothing you can take away from these pages, my message to you is to set your intentions wisely because ill will begets ill will. Follow your passions because why else are we here but to be explorative and expressive in our true element(s)? Always tell the truth, even when it hurts or is undesirable, because the truth always comes out anyway. Present as the person you want people to see in you all the time because it is always best when you are in control of your own story. You are not only the main character. You are the writer, the producer, the cameraman, and the director. Work hard at your relationships, all of them, because you never know how you affect someone else, and you need everyone in your village to be solid and for you. Do not be afraid to use your free God-given and childlike imagination to solve problems, because the simplest solutions can come when we are not so tightly wound. Exercise empathy at every possible point—it will allow you to connect with even the most distant and far-to-reach individuals. Create a self-care routine that allows you to align with your inner person so you may live more in balance and in tune with your soul for the clearest and happiest mind. Never shirk your responsibilities, because no one respects laziness. And never give up, because you will never accomplish anything by being a quitter.

So, what is your resolve?

STRENGTHEN YOUR SUPERPOWERS. ACTUALIZE YOUR PURPOSE.

How has endurance helped you reach where you are today?
How will you continue to endure in the future?
How will you encourage others to endure?

HOW TO SECURE YOUR AUTHENTICITY INSURANCE
WITH *Endurance*

The journey is most important, not the destination.

Do not let life's journey end before you have had a chance to really begin.

CONCLUSION

am honored you made it this far. Thank you for reading to the end. I know I do not have any fancy letters or degrees behind my name, except an unused finance certification, but I do have my experience and my word. I am confident I can stand firmly on both.

In under a decade, I have:

- Climbed vertically on the corporate ladder, moving seven grade levels

- Studied and earned two professional licenses, an adjuster and an agent

- Held two leadership roles in two departments on two separate sides of a company

- Managed between ten and twenty people, aging early twenties to fifties,

- Trained over fifty people

- Mentored almost ten people

- Promoted six people

- Served on three ERGs supporting the Black community, the AAPI community, and the specially-abled community

- Moderated and been in the spotlight of several DEI-charged ERG events

- Assisted in and facilitated events to boost employee engagement, connectivity, and development

- Initiated, scripted, produced, and hosted a podcast to assist employee mental health to better adapt in a newly branded high-performance environment with global distribution being posted on the company's main intranet page

- Created numerous resources to increase service effectiveness and efficiencies, allowing for total team transformations and performance improvements

- Managed projects end-to-end for organizational savings of tens of thousands of dollars, and eased teams through operational changes by building infrastructure for improved communication and support.

If this does not speak to you, I have won over twenty-one internal company awards, being recognized for quality assurance, team player, continuous improvement—making things better for both internal and external customers—top performer, and, my favorite, putting people first. And that is just my professional life.

In my personal life, I

- Owned my first car outright by twenty-three

- Was promoted to my first leadership role by twenty-four

- Bought my first house, no cosign required, at twenty-five

- Made my first six figures by twenty-six

- And finished my second book, this book, at twenty-seven.

Reading *Authenticity Insurance* hopefully has allowed you to try something new, perhaps in journaling or connecting with a newly realized purpose. What I really hope it has done is help shift the conversation to older and younger generations working together more cohesively in the workplace, sharing ideas and best practices for mutual success and development. More diverse leadership *will* make for more diverse solutions.

Authenticity Insurance was written with the purpose of reintroducing you to the tools you already have inside you. It confirms you are in control of you, and you can do whatever you want with your life and future. You must know which way you are going before you take off. Take your time and continue to reflect. Come back and reread, maybe tell a friend about this book, or start a book club. Tell your employer you want me to speak to your company and do a deep dive to help reset the culture. We must also keep the conversation about safe workplaces going and emphasize the importance of mental health for everyone to truly maximize their potential and operate at a high level.

Again, whether you are a leader in title or leader in action, it does not matter. We all have the responsibility to do the inner work on ourselves to know who is showing up every day, answering and acting on our behalf. Is it the blocked you, or is it the free you? Ask yourself the questions throughout this book as many times as you need to get to the other side. Finding your inner child, reprogramming your brain, overcoming a difficult disposition or personality, and transforming to the most authentic version of you is no easy task. Know you are not in it alone. Though this book is done, I am not even close to finished on myself, which means there will be a part two . . . and in the meantime, there is always my reflection journal on Amazon, *The Authentic Leader Journal*, to help.

I will say, though, this is the most clarity I have had my entire life. In five years, I have shed over thirty pounds. I know that is not a lot, but if you see photos, I look like a different person. After an almost twenty-year battle with my relationship with food and body image, I finally see it coming to an end. I am now capable of telling myself I can stop eating when I feel full because I am in control of where my next meal is coming from. And, on the record, I can go to work in the kitchen now after having time to practice and come to appreciate food for its purpose, which is as nourishment and a love language. The kitchen is my second home office.

In shedding physical weight, my mind, with time, became stronger. I did go through a little under ten therapists total. By the last therapist, I knew my problems. My anger, my inability to communicate well, and neglecting my mental health were keeping me from accessing *me*. How can I be authentic when I cannot see past my emotions or properly identify what they are so I can do a little processing to better articulate my needs? And communication? Communication is at the center of everything. How will people know who I am if I am unable to communicate? And how will people know or understand how to meet me where I am concerning my mental health conditions if I am incapable of expressing myself?

From the weight change to the mind change and village work, I do the work daily. I keep connected with my close friends and find myself finally having that safe "girl group" we all imagine having, watching favorites like HBO's *Sex and The City* or Amazon Prime's *Harlem*. I connect with my mentors regularly. I am on the phone with family often, checking in and ensuring they receive the energy they deserve for all the support they have provided throughout my life. For the first time in my life, things are relatively peaceful, and I can sit in my stillness without as much anxiety.

The transformation does not have to be a physical transformation, but moving into the mind could be a good start. Create a routine. Get up early every day, try 6 a.m. Exercise first. Meal prep for the day. Shower and get dressed for the day (even if you work remotely). Go to work. Go out for happy hour with friends. Read a book or watch a favorite show or movie when you come home and are turning in for the night. Meditate before you go to sleep or when you wake up, or both. Each of these represents self-care practically, physically, socially, spiritually, emotionally, and mentally.

If I had not recognized self-neglect was the missing piece, I would not have been able to take control. Self-neglect left me in such darkness. The darkness kept me from reaching my better self. It just goes to show that light really does defeat darkness. When your authentic light shines through, there will be no brighter light to illuminate your path. You will have no one able to dim you. You will be self-supporting as well as a support to others. No matter where you go, you will be spreading your light, authentically feeding the world with your positivity.

Remember, you are light. Be light. And always have and show gratitude.

ACKNOWLEDGMENTS

Thank you to everyone who read this book. I hope this book brings light to a dark world. I would be nowhere without the amazing people who make up my village or the antagonists the universe strategically placed in my life.

To my parents and grandparents, I love you all very much. Thank you for raising me as best you could and for my talents. Without you, I would not be here. Without you, I would have no one and nothing to work for. I wish to be able to return the favor of caring for you the way you have cared for me. I promise I see what you meant now about family and legacy. And for our family, I will not let anything or anyone stop me.

To my siblings, there is nothing here except love. No matter where our lives take us, I am here to be the best sister I am allowed to be, with respect to our differences in lifestyle choices. I hope when our parents are no longer with us, we can have the relationships we were all meant to have with one another. There is no way we were blessed with each other for no reason. I do believe, soon enough, we will reconnect and find the love that was always here.

To my extended family, aunts, uncles, and cousins, I hope we can reconnect more often. Life gets away from us; however, family will always be first. If I am being honest, I will probably make it my aim to reestablish a family reunion because those were fun, and why did we ever stop in the first place? Our strength is in our vast numbers. And just on Mom's side alone, we have the numbers. The only way our family will survive is together.

To my friends, thank you for always telling me to go for it, no matter the "it." You bring me joy and peace in knowing our relationships are real. To know I have people in my village I can trust means the world to me. I am grateful for every mentor session, smoke session, happy hour, movie day, spa day, holiday, you name it. I hope you feel that my love for you extends far and wide. May we continue to grow together.

To my work team (The Steady Eddies, my peers, my leaders, my mentors, etc.), thank you for trusting me and for every ounce of effort you put forth daily. You all inspire me daily to log into work. You keep me going. You helped me find my purpose in realizing how much I want to help people develop into the best version of themselves. You motivate me to keep growing. You make it worthwhile to keep going.

To my partner, thank you for being a safeguard.

Thank you for being the fire to melt the ice around my heart.

Your eyes are captivating.

Quite the vision you have always kept.

Your big brain is beautiful.

Being inspired by your character, my soul has wept.

Your hands are pure gold.

I do not want to imagine what life would be like if we had not met.

Thank you for your grounding.

Thank you for your patience.

Thank you for your loving kindness.

Thank you for your common sense.

Your strength is enduring.

Your wisdom others cannot circumvent.

Your talent is never-ending.

Your heart is beyond compassionate.

There is no doubt in my mind that if I was "made" for any man, it was you.

I love that you are mine. United, there is nothing we cannot do.

Thank you for being here for the ride.

May we continue to grow with time and age together like fine wine.

Love, Kitty
The Mother of Our Legacy

The
Authenticity
SESSIONS

The
Authentic
LEADER JOURNAL

Love
AUTHENTICALLEE

Learn more about LoveAuthenticallee,
The Authentic Leader Journal, and The Authenticity Sessions at
www.loveauthenticallee.org

The Authentic Leader Journal Now Available on Amazon
https://a.co/d/37NLlzv
Visit the Amazon page here:

#womanowned
#familyowned
#blackowned
#supportsmallbusinesses
#loveauthenticallee
#authenticleadership

Printed by Libri Plureos GmbH in Hamburg,
Germany